THE BOOK OF THE JEWISH LIFE

JO DAVID
and
DANIEL B. SYME

UAHC PRESS
NEW YORK, NEW YORK

For my husband, Neil Yerman, my *aleph* through *tav*.
For my father, Stan Marx ל״ז, who ignited my love of literature.
For my grandmother, Bessie Steinberg ל״ז, whose stories linked me forever to tradition.

JO DAVID

For my son, Joshua.

DANIEL B. SYME

Library of Congress Cataloging-in-Publication Data

David, Jo.
The book of the Jewish life / Jo David and Daniel B. Syme.
p.   cm.
Includes bibliographical references and index.
Summary: A text on Jewish life as it is lived today with each chapter describing a stage or milestone of that life including traditional practices and modern observances.
ISBN 0-8074-0628-7 (paperback: alk. paper)
1. Judaism—Customs and practices—Juvenile literature. 2. Life cycle, Human—Religious aspects—Judaism—Juvenile literature.
[1. Judaism—Customs and practices. 2. Life cycle, Human—Religious aspects—Judaism.]
I. Syme, Daniel B. II. Title.
BM700. D397   1997
296.7—dc21   97-15824
                                                                 CIP
                                                                  AC

This book is printed on acid-free paper.
Copyright © 1997 by the UAHC Press
Book design by Itzhack Shelomi
Manufactured in the United States of America
10 9 8 7 6 5 4 3 2 1

CONTENTS

PICTURE CREDITS

ACKNOWLEDGMENTS

The idea for this book was born in the social hall of the Jewish Family Congregation in South Salem, New York, approximately ten years ago, after Rabbi Jo David's husband, artist Neil Yerman, had just completed a presentation to the congregation on the artistic character of Jewish life-cycle documents. Aron Hirt-Manheimer, former acquisitions editor for the UAHC Press and present editor of *Reform Judaism* magazine, was a member of that congregation. Aron introduced himself and suggested that Neil write a book for the lower grades on the subject of the Jewish life cycle. After some discussion, it was agreed that the book would be written by Rabbi Jo David. As it took shape, Rabbi Daniel B. Syme was asked to participate in its development because of his writings on Jewish life, many of which are contained in Rabbi Syme's *The Jewish Home*.

Since the book's inception, many people have contributed to the development and production of this book.

Aron Hirt-Manheimer strongly supported the initial concept and was tremendously helpful in fleshing out the early drafts. Rabbi Bernard M. Zlotowitz reviewed the manuscript for content and accuracy. His helpful recommendations were a constant source of inspiration and wisdom. Textbook editor David P. Kasakove was especially responsible for giving the manuscript its present form. Our thanks go to him for his perseverance, mentoring, and support. Rabbi Steven M. Rosman was a fountain of stories and ideas. His contribution is evident in many of the stories that open each chapter.

During the writing of this book, a decision was reached to invite Reform rabbis, educators, and interested lay people to participate in the book's creation. A text-only version of the contents was printed with a questionnaire in *Compass*, a publication of the UAHC Department of Education, Spring 1996. The overwhelming and meaningful responses provided informed suggestions, many of which have been incorporated into the text. Our thanks, therefore, are extended to all of these respondents and to Alayne Zatulove, who volunteered to summarize and analyze the results of the returned questionnaires.

We wish to thank members of the UAHC Press, particularly Annette Abramson, Stuart L. Benick, Bennett Lovett-Graff, Rabbi Ellen Nemhauser, Alex Ralph, Seymour Rossel, Greg Sanders, Cara Schlesinger, and Elyn Wollensky, all of whom were exemplary in their efforts to see this project through to completion. We also want to thank the many institutions and individuals that permitted us to reprint their photographs and artwork, particularly Rabbi Bradley Bleefeld and the Jewish Heritage Calendar Company.

As a final note, this book was the result of years of teaching in Reform religious schools, where many of the topics that appear in this book were developed. Our thanks, therefore, go to the many children who participated in the field testing of this material, as well as to the rabbis and religious school principals who supported this work. A special thanks is owed to those at Temple Shaaray Tefila, New York City; Temple Chaverim, Plainview, New York; Temple Emanuel, Great Neck, New York; and B'nai Elohim, Scarsdale, New York.

Finally, we must thank our families for their love, their support, and their patience.

JO DAVID AND DANIEL B. SYME
MAY 1997

From Generation to Generation...

Salman Chernin's bar mitzvah photo, 1919.

The Chernin family portrait, taken shortly after the family's arrival in America, 1909. Channa, seated on the far left, is shown with her husband, Schepschel; an unidentified relative; and the family children: Rivka, Abraham, Scheina, and Zelda (standing); Perla, Salman, Feigl, and Lila (sitting in the bottom row).

The Chernin family passport, used to travel from Russia to New York, 1909.

A LIGHT OF GOD IS THE SOUL OF MAN

IN LOVING MEMORY OF
MY BELOVED
Mother
Anna   Chernin

Died   Dec. 27

1930

חנה רחל טשערנין
נפטרה ז׳ - טבת - תר״ף

God Rest her Soul in Peace

YEAR	DAY	DATE	MONTH
1933	Thursday	5	Jan.
1933	Monday	25	Dec.
1934	Thursday	13	Dec.
1936	Thursday	2	Jan.
1936	Monday	21	Dec.
1937	Saturday	11	Dec.
1938	Thursday	29	Dec.
1939	Tuesday	19	Dec.

YEAR	DAY	DATE	MONTH
1952	Thursday	25	Dec.
1953	Sunday	13	Dec.
1955	Saturday	1	Jan.
1955	Thursday	22	Dec.
1956	Tuesday	11	Dec.
1957	Monday	30	Dec.
1958	Thursday	18	Dec.
1960	Thursday	7	Jan.
1960	Monday	26	Dec.
1961	Thursday	14	Dec.
1963	Thursday	3	Jan.
1963	Monday	23	Dec.
1964	Saturday	12	Dec.
1965	Thursday	30	Dec.
1966	Tuesday	20	Dec.
1968	Monday	8	Jan.
1968	Saturday	28	Dec.
1969	Tuesday	16	Dec.
1971	Monday	4	Jan.
1971	Saturday	25	Dec.

BREW RELIGIOUS SUPPLIES, 41-43 DELANCEY ST., NEW YORK   Tel. Dry Dock 8437

The yahrzeit calendar memorializing Channa's death.

Feigl, who died in 1992, stands by the grave of her mother, Channa.

CHAPTER ONE

CYCLES FROM GENERATION TO GENERATION

A Tree for David

Once upon a time, a young woman was walking down a road in a small village. It was a beautiful day, and she was enjoying the flowers and the trees and the people going to and fro.

In front of one of the houses, she saw a very strange sight. A very old man with a long white beard was digging a hole in the ground. He was so old and so frail

that it was a wonder he could stand up, much less bend over and dig in the dirt.

The young woman walked closer to him to see exactly what he was doing.

On the ground next to him was a small sapling, its roots wrapped in a burlap bag. It was a very small sapling, not quite as high as a tulip. As the young woman watched, the old man very gently placed the roots of the sapling into the hole he had dug and covered them with earth.

"Excuse me, sir," said the young woman. "My name is Rachel. Do you mind if I ask what you are doing? It's so hot out here, and you are so old. Shouldn't you be sitting somewhere in the shade?"

Slowly the old man finished covering the roots of the sapling and then straightened up. He looked at the woman and said, "Can't you see? I've just finished planting a tree."

"Planting a tree?" asked Rachel. "Why did you plant a tree? Especially such a small one. You're a very old man. You'll never have any pleasure from that tree. It won't be tall enough to give shade to anyone for many years."

The old man looked at her, a

peaceful expression on his face. "You don't understand," the old man said. "I'm planting this tree for David."

"Is David your son?" she asked.

"Oh, no," laughed the old man. "My son is an old man himself. He won't see this tree full grown either."

"Is David your grandson?"

"No," said the old man. "My grandson's name is Nathan."

"Is David your great-grandson?"

"No, my great-grandson's name is Benjamin."

"I don't understand," said Rachel. "If David is not your son or your grandson or your great-grandson, who is David?"

"I am David," said the old man. "And David will also be my great-great-grandson—when he's born. I know that my remaining time on earth is very short. By the time David is born, I'll be gone. But I know he will be named after me so I'm planting this tree for him. It's a tradition in our family.

"Do you see that tall oak over there? That was planted by my great-great-grandfather, David, for me. When I was small, the tree was small; but we grew up together, just as my David and this tree will grow. Hopefully, one day, David will plant a tree for his great-great-grandson."

"Thank you," said the young woman, and she began to leave.

"Wait," said the old man. "It's very hot. Would you like to sit under my big tree and have some lemonade?"

"No, thank you," said the woman as she hurried away. "I can't take the time now. I have to go and plant a tree for Rachel."

BASED ON A TALMUDIC LEGEND

What Is a Cycle?

A cycle is the time during which an event or series of events occurs. Some cycles are longer than others. A minute is a cycle of sixty seconds; a day is a cycle of twenty-four hours; a year is a cycle of twelve months. The continuous flow of the seasons is also a cycle. Every time spring comes, a new cycle begins. Living things have cycles, too. Many trees have yearly cycles. In spring, new buds appear on the branches. In late spring and early summer, leaves appear. In fall, the leaves drop to the ground, and in winter, the branches are bare. Then, when spring comes again, a new cycle of growth begins again for the tree.

In the Book of Ecclesiastes, we read a beautiful poem about cycles.

To every thing there is a season, and a
    time to every purpose under the
    heaven:
A time to be born, and a time to die;
A time to plant, and a time to harvest
    that which is planted;
A time to slay, and a time to heal;
A time to tear down, and a time to
    build up;
A time to weep, and a time to laugh;
A time to wail, and a time to dance;
A time to throw stones, and a time to
    gather stones;
A time to embrace, and a time to refrain
    from embracing;
A time to seek, and a time to lose;
A time to keep, and a time to discard;
A time to rip, and a time to sew;
A time to be silent, and a time to speak;
A time to love, and a time to hate;
A time for war, and a time for peace.

ECCLESIASTES 3:1–8

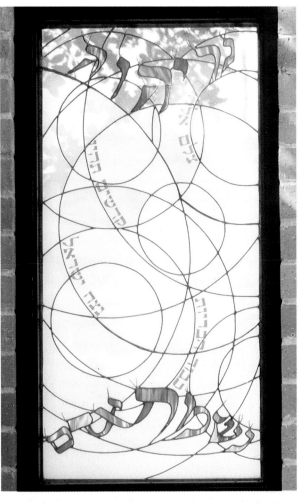

This Plachte-Zuieback art glass window evokes the cyclical character of Judaism.

Life Cycles— A Special Type of Cycle

People experience different cycles in their lives. Some cycles occur daily, some monthly, and some once a year or every few years.

In Judaism, we emphasize the importance of adults passing on responsibility to younger people. A special Hebrew phrase for this concept, *ledor vador* לְדוֹר וָדוֹר, means "from generation to generation." Some actions we take during our lives were taken by our parents, grandparents, and even great-grandparents before us. The repetition of these actions is a type of cycle. When these actions are connected to specific times in our lives, we call them "life-cycle events." There are life-cycle events that many Jews have in common. With most of these events, there are rituals to celebrate them.

Four plates painted in 1751 depict (clockwise from top left) a Sabbath celebration; preparations for a Berit Milah; a wedding; and a father bringing his child into a synagogue.

Birth

- Naming ceremony
- *Berit Bat* or *Berit Milah* ceremony

Beginning of Jewish Education

- Consecration ceremony
- Presentation of new books and religious items, such as a Bible or prayer book

Beginning of Jewish Adulthood (usually about thirteen years of age)

- Bar or bat mitzvah ceremony
- Celebration with family and community

Completion of Formal Jewish Studies

- Confirmation ceremony
- Receiving a certificate of completion
- *Siyum* (Hebrew word for a completion party)

Living a Jewish Life

- Saying *Shehecheyanu* for new beginnings
- Affixing a *mezuzah*
- Giving *tzedakah* from your earnings
- Joining a temple

Conversion to Judaism (This is a special life-cycle event for non-Jews who decide to become Jews.)

- Detailed study of Jewish history and religious practices
- Religious ceremonies and celebrations to mark the commitment to Judaism
- *Mikveh* (ritual immersion)
- Circumcision or *hatafat dam berit* for men

Jewish Marriage

- Engagement
- *Kiddushin* (marriage ceremony, which entails many specific rituals)
- *Sheva Berachot* before ritual meal

Death

- Preparation of the body for burial
- Funeral or memorial service
- Burial
- Mourning customs: *shivah, yahrzeit,* and *Yizkor*

Repeating Life-Cycle Rituals—Introducing Generations

An important characteristic of the life cycle is that its steps occur in one generation after another. The word *generation* is used to describe people born within a specific twenty-year period. Your parents belong to one generation; you and your siblings, your brothers and sisters, belong to the next generation; and your own children and your siblings' children will be the generation after yours.

Most special events in the life cycle occur in every generation. Your father, mother, and their siblings may have cele-

brated bar or bat mitzvah בַּר/בַּת מִצְוָה in their generation. When you and your sister, brother, or cousins celebrate bar or bat mitzvah, you will be experiencing this momentous occasion for your generation.

GENERATION 1	Your parents
GENERATION 2	You—Your siblings (brothers and sisters)
GENERATION 3	Your children—Your brothers' and your sisters' children

A bat mitzvah draws together the generations.

Putting Generations and Life Cycles Together

Having been introduced to the concepts of life-cycle rituals and generations, you are now ready to see how they combine to affect your life.

Some families have their own unique life-cycle rituals or customs. Have you ever wondered why your family always sings a certain song on a wedding anniversary or why your parents use only certain candles for a birthday cake? These are *your* family's rituals or customs. Other families may pass down a *talit* טַלִּת from genera-tion to generation at the time of bar or bat mitzvah or give a wedding gift of Shabbat candlesticks that have been in the family for a long time. A common family life-cycle ritual is to name a child for a special relative.

We do not often give much thought to the way we observe life-cycle celebra-tions. We perform them in a certain man-ner because our family has performed them that way for a long time. Yet these rituals were begun generations ago by family members we may not even have met.

Knowing more about past family gener-ations and how they celebrated the steps in their lives may help you understand how and why these customs have devel-oped. Through this knowledge, you may develop new life-cycle rituals of your own.

A family at a Jewish resort in upstate New York, ca. 1910.

Genealogy— Mapping Family Generations

Genealogy is the study of the generations of one's family. In its most basic form, a family tree is a picture that shows the relationships in a particular family. Some family trees are very simple, showing the relationships within only a small part of the family. Other trees are more complex, listing the places where people were born and died and other information about them.

The following family tree is a simple version, showing the official beginning of the Jewish people.

Abraham's Family Tree

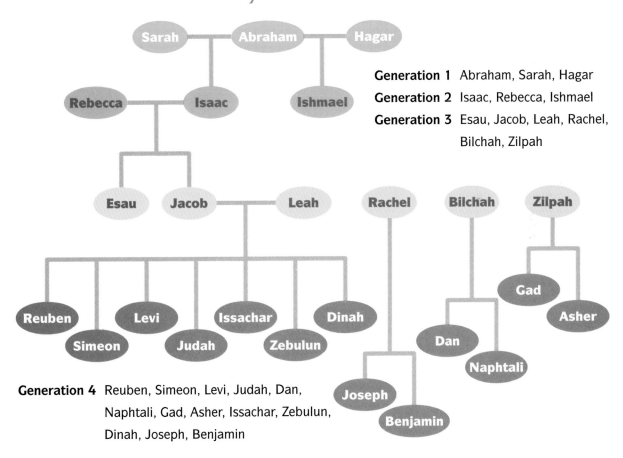

Generation 1 Abraham, Sarah, Hagar
Generation 2 Isaac, Rebecca, Ishmael
Generation 3 Esau, Jacob, Leah, Rachel, Bilchah, Zilpah

Generation 4 Reuben, Simeon, Levi, Judah, Dan, Naphtali, Gad, Asher, Issachar, Zebulun, Dinah, Joseph, Benjamin

nderstanding about cycles and generations helps us see that the way we live, especially the way we live as Jews, makes us part of a large, international community. By using Jewish rituals to celebrate life-cycle events, we feel connected to other Jews of our generation and to generations of our Jewish ancestors.

When we teach our own children Jewish ways of celebrating key moments in the life cycle, we are participating in the special Jewish tradition of *ledor vador*, "from generation to generation." This tradition of handing down Jewish teachings and rituals from one generation to another has helped keep Judaism alive for thousands of years.

In this chapter you explored the Jewish life cycle and rituals. In the next chapter you will look at birth and explore the Jewish life-cycle rituals that mark the arrival of a new child into the Jewish community.

A family tree, covering the years 1801 to 1945.

It's Easy If You Know the Secret

When the world was very new, Adam and Eve had the difficult job of naming all things in the Garden of Eden. No one had ever named things before, and it was very difficult.

One day, for example, Adam and Eve came upon a great rush of falling water. Adam looked at the crashing curtain of water and said confidently, "I think we should call this a volcano."

Eve looked at him and shook her head vigorously. "A volcano? I think a volcano is something that's hot and shoots up. This water is cold and is falling down. I think we should call this a waterfall."

Adam was sure the thing should be called a volcano.

Eve was sure it should be called a waterfall. They argued for hours, but they just couldn't agree. Finally Adam said, "This is a hard thing to name. Let's find something easier." So off they went.

Later that day, Adam and Eve came across a huge four-footed creature with a bushy mane. It was tan-colored, and a loud, scary sound came from its mouth. Eve looked at the creature and with great assurance and authority said, "Oh, Adam! What a wonderful whale!"

"Whale?" said Adam, scornfully. "That's not a whale. A whale should look like something that lives in an ocean. That's obviously a lion because when it's not hunting for food, it's 'lyin'' around in the sun. Besides, 'lion' sounds majestic, and this animal looks like the king of beasts."

"But I just know it's a whale," insisted Eve. "Nope. Lion," said Adam.

Again they argued and argued. God heard them and became very annoyed. Adam and Eve heard a loud rumbling in the sky. It was God.

"Children! Children! Why are you arguing? What's the matter?" God asked. "Adam doesn't know how to name anything," said Eve.

"Eve doesn't know how to name anything," said Adam.

"But you both are doing a very good job naming things," said God. "'Waterfall' is a wonderful name for water that's falling down. And 'lion' is a terrific name for a majestic beast that spends a lot of time lying in the sun. A good name tells you something special about the thing you have named. If you remember that, you won't go wrong." Suddenly it was quiet in the Garden of Eden. "Waterfall," said Adam. "Lion," said Eve.

They smiled at each other. Naming is easy if you know the secret.

BASED ON "EVE'S DIARY," MARK TWAIN

What's in a Name?

We do not come into this world with a little nametag attached to our wrists. Before we are born, our parents have already begun to think about choosing our names. We learn very quickly to respond to those names. Only later do we begin to wonder why our parents chose a particular name. As we get older, most of us use that name or some variation of it.

A famous Jewish saying states:

Every person has three names: the name given by parents, the name assigned by others, and the name one makes for oneself.

ECCLESIASTES RABBAH VII 1:3

What exactly does this saying mean? Your parents call you by the name they gave you at birth (e.g., Joseph or Rachel). Your friends may call you by another name (e.g., Joe or Shelly or even a nickname that's totally different from your original name). When you reach adulthood, the name you acquire may be a name that describes your position in life (e.g., mom, dad, doctor, rabbi, senator, teacher, or coach).

Years ago, most people were identified by their first name and the name of either their father or mother (e.g., Simon ben Ari), by the name of the place where they lived (e.g., Rachel Hamburg), or by their occupation (e.g., Joseph Blacksmith).

Traditionally, Jews were given two different first names if they lived in a country where the local spoken language was not Hebrew. A person was still given a Hebrew name that included the name of his or her parents. But that person was also given another name in the commonly spoken language of the country.

This "double-naming" system came about because Diaspora Jews (Jews living outside Israel) felt that their lives would be less complicated if their names were more common and more easily pronounceable. Therefore, a child born in an English-speaking country would be given an English name and a child born in a French-speaking country, a French name. Moses, who grew up in Egypt, had an Egyptian name. Mordecai and Esther had Babylonian names because Babylonian was the commonly spoken language of Persia, where they lived.

However, tradition dictates that each Jewish child should have a Hebrew name that links him or her to the Jewish people. Our Hebrew names are used when we participate in Jewish ceremonies and life-cycle rituals.

TEXT STUDY

Names have special meanings. The Bible teaches that our given names are significant because they help us understand many things about ourselves. Below are a few examples of names from the Bible:

Genesis 2:7 *Adonai Eloheinu* formed man from the dust of the earth.

This man was called Adam, from the Hebrew word *adamah*, which means "earth."

Genesis 3:20 The man [Adam] named his wife Eve because she was the mother of all the living.

In Hebrew, Eve is *Chavah*, from the word for "life."

"Your name shall no longer be Jacob, but Israel, for you have striven with beings divine and human, and have prevailed" (Genesis 32:29).

Genesis 17:5 And God said to Abram, "And you shall no longer be called Abram, but your name shall be Abraham, for I make you the father of a multitude of nations."

In Hebrew, Abraham is *Avraham*, which combines the words for "father" and "many people."

Genesis 17:15-16 And God said to Abraham, "As for your wife Sarai, you shall not call her Sarai, but her name shall be Sarah.... I will bless her so that she shall give rise to nations; rulers of peoples shall come from her."

The name *Sarah* means "princess." Sarah received her name when God promised that this princess would give rise to rulers of peoples.

Genesis 21:5-6 Now Abraham was a hundred years old when his son Isaac was born to him [and Sarah]. Sarah said, "God has brought me laughter; everyone who hears will laugh with me."

In Hebrew, the name Isaac is *Yitzchak*, from the Hebrew root for "laughter." Perhaps Sarah was filled with so much laughter and joy as a result of having a child that she named him *Yitzchak*.

Exodus 2:5,6,10 The daughter of Pharaoh came down to bathe in the Nile, while her maidens walked along the Nile. She spied the basket among the

Adam Naming the Creation, *a 1900 engraving.*

reeds and sent her slave girl to fetch it. When she opened it, she saw that it was a child, a boy crying.... She named him Moses, explaining, "I drew him out of the water."

The Hebrew word for Moses is *Mosheh*, which means "who draws out."

Many parents choose names that indicate their desires for their children. The girl's name Naomi, from the Hebrew word *naim*, means "beautiful" or "pleasant." Parents who name their daughter Naomi are expressing the wish that their daughter will be beautiful. Other parents may name their son *Ari*, which means "lion," hoping that their son will grow up to be a courageous person.

Choosing a Hebrew Name

There is no one "right way" to choose a Hebrew name. Different customs within the Jewish community may influence parents' choices. Among Ashkenazic Jews, who trace their roots to Central and Eastern European countries, the custom is to name children in memory of a close relative who is no longer living. Sephardic Jews, who trace their roots to Mediterranean countries, especially Spain and Portugal, name their children in honor of a living relative.

Some parents choose an English name that begins with the same letter as the name of a relative, especially when the relative is of a sex different from that of the new baby. In some cases, both the Hebrew and English names come from the name of the relative; in other cases, parents use only the corresponding Hebrew name or only the corresponding English name. Some parents turn to books of English and Hebrew names for help. Some do not give their children any Hebrew name. However, it is never too late to get a Hebrew name. With the help of your parents, rabbi, or teacher, you can select one for yourself.

A Guide to Special Situations: What If...

- **you were never given a Hebrew name?** Talk to your parents, then to your teacher or rabbi. It's never too late to get a Hebrew name. You can select a Hebrew equivalent of your English name or choose a different Hebrew name that means something special. You and other classmates who are choosing Hebrew names for the first time may want to arrange a special naming ceremony.

- **a parent doesn't have a Hebrew name?** Perhaps your parent would like to choose a Hebrew name and participate in the naming ceremony.

- **a parent isn't Jewish?** Your name consists of your Hebrew name and the Hebrew name of your Jewish parent. It is also possible to add the English name of your non-Jewish parent.

- **a parent is a convert to Judaism?** A parent who converted to Judaism has a Hebrew name. As part of the conversion process, converts chose a Hebrew name for themselves.

Jewish Naming Ceremonies and Certificates

Receiving a Hebrew name is a very important event in a person's life. Naming usually takes place during either a synagogue ceremony or a special home ceremony, held soon after the baby's birth.

A child-naming ceremony at a synagogue usually takes place at a Friday evening or Saturday morning Shabbat service after the baby is born, when both the mother and baby can be present. The parents and the baby are called up to the ark. This ceremony may take place during the Torah תּוֹרָה service with parents chanting a blessing for the Torah reading. The rabbi may make a few brief comments. Then the child is blessed, and the Hebrew name is announced.

Many congregations give the parents a naming certificate with the child's Hebrew name. A Hebrew-naming certificate is different from a birth certificate. Ask your parents to show you your birth certificate. You will notice it is undecorated. A Hebrew-naming certificate, on the other hand, is often very colorful because receiving a Hebrew name is a joyous and happy occasion.

A Berit Bat *ceremony.*

There are two other types of ceremonies during which a Jewish child can receive a Hebrew name: a *Berit Milah* בְּרִית מִילָה for boys and a *Berit Bat* בְּרִית בַּת for girls. Both ceremonies can be performed in addition to the naming ceremony in the synagogue. *Berit Milah* and *Berit Bat* will be explained in the next chapter.

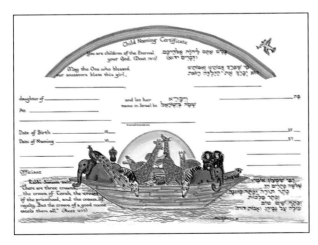

A contemporary child-naming certificate, designed by Neil Yerman.

17

There are several blessings that are often said during a naming ceremony. Shehecheyanu שֶׁהֶחֱיָנוּ is a blessing said for a new beginning. A naming ceremony is one of many occasions when it is appropriate to say the Shehecheyanu.

בָּרוּךְ אַתָּה, יְיָ אֱלֹהֵינוּ, מֶלֶךְ הָעוֹלָם, שֶׁהֶחֱיָנוּ וְקִיְּמָנוּ וְהִגִּיעָנוּ לַזְּמַן הַזֶּה.

We praise You, Adonai our God, Ruler of the universe, who has kept us alive, sustained us, and brought us to this joyous time.

When a naming ceremony takes place at the time of a Torah reading, a blessing called *Mi Sheberach* מִי שֶׁבֵּרַךְ is often said.

For a boy

מִי שֶׁבֵּרַךְ אֲבוֹתֵינוּ, אַבְרָהָם, יִצְחָק וְיַעֲקֹב, וְאִמּוֹתֵינוּ, שָׂרָה, רִבְקָה, רָחֵל וְלֵאָה, הוּא יְבָרֵךְ אֶת־הַיֶּלֶד הָרַךְ הַנִּמּוֹל וִירַפֵּא אוֹתוֹ רְפוּאָה שְׁלֵמָה. וְיִזְכּוּ אָבִיו וְאִמּוֹ לְגַדְּלוֹ, לְחַנְּכוֹ וּלְחַכְּמוֹ. וְיִהְיוּ יָדָיו וְלִבּוֹ לְאֵל אֱמוּנָה, וְנֹאמַר אָמֵן.

May God who blessed our ancestors, Abraham, Isaac, and Jacob; Sarah, Rebecca, Rachel, and Leah, bless this infant who has been circumcised and bring him speedily to full healing. May his father and mother have the privilege of raising him, educating him, and encouraging him to attain wisdom. May his hands and his heart be faithful in serving God. And let us all say Amen.

For a girl

מִי שֶׁבֵּרַךְ אֲבוֹתֵינוּ, אַבְרָהָם, יִצְחָק וְיַעֲקֹב, וְאִמּוֹתֵינוּ, שָׂרָה, רִבְקָה, רָחֵל וְלֵאָה, הוּא יְבָרֵךְ אֶת־הַיַּלְדָּה הָרַכָּה הַזֹּאת. וְיִזְכּוּ אָבִיהָ וְאִמָּהּ לְגַדְּלָהּ, לְחַנְּכָהּ וּלְחַכְּמָהּ. וְיִהְיוּ יָדֶיהָ וְלִבָּהּ לְאֵל אֱמוּנָה, וְנֹאמַר אָמֵן.

May God who blessed our ancestors, Abraham, Isaac, and Jacob; Sarah, Rebecca, Rachel, and Leah, bless this infant. May her father and mother have the privilege of raising her, educating her, and encouraging her to attain wisdom. May her hands and her heart be faithful in serving God. And let us all say Amen.

Birkat Hagomel בִּרְכַּת הַגּוֹמֵל is another blessing that may be said at a naming ceremony. It is a prayer traditionally said by a new mother after she has given birth.

בָּרוּךְ אַתָּה, יְיָ אֱלֹהֵינוּ, מֶלֶךְ הָעוֹלָם, הַגּוֹמֵל לַחַיָּבִים טוֹבוֹת, שֶׁגְּמָלַנִי כָּל טוֹב.

Blessed is Adonai our God, Ruler of the universe, who deals kindly with the undeserving and who has dealt kindly with me.

SUMMARY

In this chapter we learn that Jews have a tradition from biblical times of carefully choosing their children's names. Now we know why many of us have both secular and Hebrew names, which we use at different times in our lives and for different occasions. We have formal naming ceremonies during which most of us receive the Hebrew names that help connect us to the rest of the Jewish community. In the next chapter we shall further investigate those ceremonies.

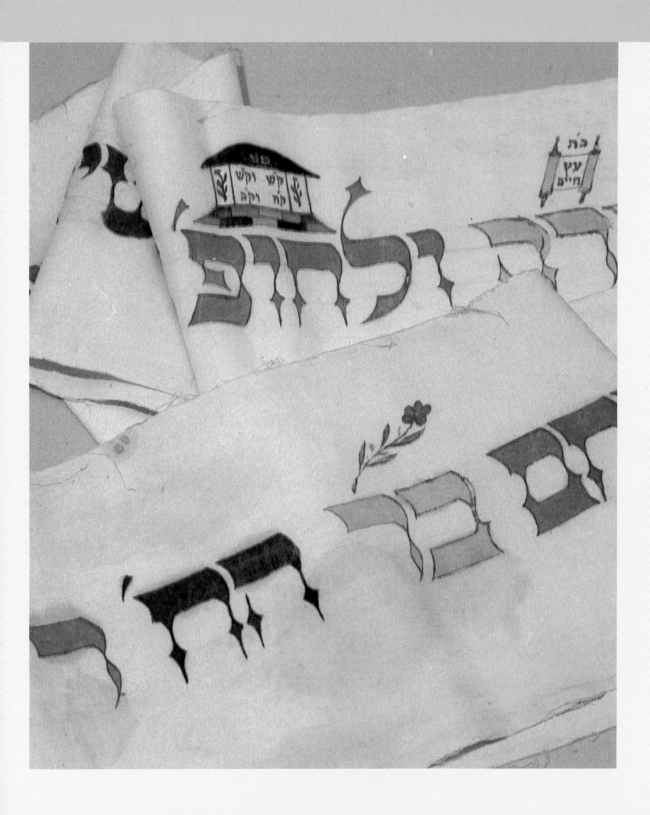

For the Sake of the Children

When was Moses coming down from that mountain? Some people thought he must have died. How could anyone survive up there for so many days without food or water?

"Aaron, when is your brother, Moses, coming down from Mount Sinai?" asked Reuven.

"If he's dead, who will lead us out of this wilderness?" asked Devorah.

"Aaron, you must give the orders now. Your brother is not coming down," said Benjamin.

"That's enough! That's enough!" shouted Aaron. "My brother is not dead. Do you hear me? He's not dead. Once God has given him the Torah, he will return to us."

"Yes, but when will that be?" asked Leah. "We cannot wait here in the desert forever."

Just then, thunder erupted from the mountaintop, echoing throughout the valley below.

"What was that?" they shouted.

The thunder rumbled again, and the Israelites stopped shouting. They looked up to the mountain and saw Moses standing before them on a cliff.

"Moses," the people cried, "you have returned to us. Show us God's Torah. Bring it down here for us to see."

"I have no Torah to show you," declared Moses. "God heard your whining and your complaining. How could God entrust the Torah to you? I must give God something to prove that we are worthy of the honor of receiving God's Teaching."

"Here, Moses. Take my gold earrings and my emerald necklace," called out one woman.

"Yes, Moses. Here is my ring and these silver coins," called out one of the men.

Soon all the Israelites were offering Moses the jewels they had gotten from the Egyptians when they fled from Egypt.

Moses took the jewels and disappeared into the heights of Mount Sinai. This time he was not gone for days. He was back very quickly and stood on the cliff with the jewels still in his hands.

"God does not want your jewels," said Moses. "All your gold and silver are not worth God's Torah."

"Then ask if God will give us the Torah because of the deeds of our ancestors, Abraham, Isaac, and Jacob."

Moses returned to the mountaintop. Again he was very quick to reappear before the Israelites.

"The deeds of our ancestors are not enough," said Moses.

"What shall we do?" cried the people. "What do we have that will convince God to trust us with the Torah?"

Standing up above the crowd, Moses could hear the mumbling of the people, trying to find a solution. He waited a long time.

Finally, one woman approached him and said: "Moses, our most precious possessions are our children. We will promise to teach the Torah to our children. We will raise them to love it and live by it. Ask God if this makes us worthy."

Moses ascended the mountain. Just as before, he returned quickly. The people were anxious. They were nervous. Would God accept this last offer?

"Yes," said Moses. "God has said that for the sake of the children, you will receive the Torah. Now you must teach it to them so that it will be inscribed upon their hearts, their minds, and their souls."

Moses placed the Torah in its own special ark. From that day on, the Torah has gone wherever we have gone. It still rests in its own special ark, our holy ark.

ADAPTED FROM SIDRAH STORIES,
STEVEN M. ROSMAN, UAHC PRESS, 1989

What Is a Berit?

God gave the Torah to the Jews at Mount Sinai in exchange for their promise to teach Torah to their children and to all future generations. When a child is born into the Jewish community, not only do we celebrate, but we also repeat this promise.

When you entered the world, you came as a blessing to your parents, their relatives, and their friends. Your circle of family and friends made phone calls, sent cards, and gave presents. All because you, this great delight, were born.

Your birth was also a blessing to the Jewish people and was probably marked by special ceremonies created for the occasion. The ceremony for welcoming a baby into the Jewish community is called a *berit* בְּרִית ceremony. *Berit* literally means "covenant." A covenant is a contract or agreement between two or more parties. Jewish parents arrange *berit* ceremonies for their children in order to remember and renew the agreement—or covenant—between God and the Jewish people at Mount Sinai.

Berit Milah— A Welcoming Ceremony for Boys

Berit Milah means "Covenant of Circumcision." During the *Berit Milah* ceremony a baby boy joins the Jewish community by being circumcised and receiving a Hebrew name. In a circumcision, the foreskin of the child's penis is surgically removed by a *mohel* מוֹהֵל or *mohelet* מוֹהֶלֶת.

While many different groups of people practiced circumcision in biblical times, circumcision for these groups was generally linked with reaching the age of puberty, usually at about the age of thirteen. Ishmael, Abraham's first son, was thirteen when he was circumcised

Circumcision, K. Felsenhardt, 1894, colored chalk drawing and gouache. S. Kirschstein Collection. Photography by Lelo Carter.

(Genesis 17:25). This may have been mentioned in the Torah to show that Jews knew about this custom. However, by changing the age of circumcision to eight days, Jews took a common custom and transformed it into a religious ritual that reflected their covenant with God.

Throughout our history, Jews have diligently fulfilled the *mitzvah* מִצְוָה, "commandment," of *Berit Milah*. When tyrants tried to outlaw the practice as a means of persecuting the Jews, we defied the ban against performing *Berit Milah*. One such tyrant was the Greek-Syrian King Antiochus, who banned *Berit Milah* in 168 B.C.E. When the Jews learned of this and other bans against Jewish religious practices, they revolted against the king and his army. Although Antiochus' army was much larger and better equipped, the Jews, led by Judah Maccabee, triumphed. The story of this amazing victory is retold every Chanukah חֲנֻכָּה.

The *Berit Milah* ceremony takes place eight days after birth. If the baby has any health problems, the ceremony is delayed until the baby is completely well. Other than health problems, two other circumstances may delay a *Berit Milah*: If the baby is adopted and his birth parents are not Jewish, his *Berit Milah* may be scheduled anytime after his birth. However, it is recommended that the *Berit Milah* take place when the baby is as young as possible. The other case for delay occurs when an adult male converts to Judaism.

A *Berit Milah* ceremony can take place in the home, in the synagogue, or in the hospital. It is traditional to perform it in the presence of a *minyan* מִנְיָן, a "quorum of ten adult Jews." Often *Berit Milah* is followed by a celebration to welcome a new member into the community.

According to Jewish law, the baby's father or a representative performs the circumcision. Today circumcisions are usually performed by a specially trained person called a *mohel* or *mohelet*. In some cases a surgeon performs the circumcision with a rabbi present to conduct the religious ritual. There are Jewish doctors now being trained as *mohalim* מוֹהֲלִים and *mohalot* מוֹהֲלוֹת (plurals of *mohel* and *mohelet*).

Today it is common practice for most

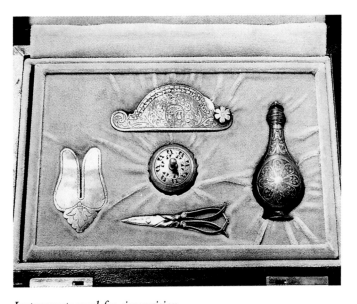

Instruments used for circumcision.

baby boys born in the Western world to be circumcised, regardless of their religion. For Jews, however, *Berit Milah* is more than circumcision. It is a unique way of welcoming newborn boys into the Jewish community with prayers of thanksgiving and celebration.

TEXT STUDY

Berit Milah is first mentioned in the Torah when God speaks to Abraham about establishing a covenant.

Abram threw himself on his face, as God spoke to him further, "As for Me, this is My covenant with you: You shall be the father of a multitude of nations. And you shall no longer be called Abram, but your name shall be Abraham, for I make you the father of a multitude of nations. I will make you exceedingly fertile and make nations of you; and kings shall come forth from you. I will maintain My covenant between Me and you, and your offspring to come, as an everlasting covenant throughout the ages, to be God to you and to your offspring to come. I give the land you sojourn in to you and your offspring to come, all the land of Canaan, as an everlasting possession. I will be their God."

God further said to Abraham, "As for you, you and your offspring to come throughout the ages shall keep My covenant. Such shall be the covenant between Me and you and your offspring to follow that you shall keep: Every male among you shall be circumcised. You shall circumcise the flesh of your foreskin, and that shall be the sign of the covenant between Me and you. And throughout the generations, every male among you shall be circumcised at the age of eight days."

GENESIS 17:3-12

Berit Bat– A Welcoming Ceremony for Girls

We have now studied how we welcome baby boys into the Jewish community. What about baby girls? After all, God gave the Torah to the Jews at Sinai for the sake of *all* Jewish children. Traditionally, the arrival of a baby girl into a Jewish family is marked by giving the father the honor of being called up to the Torah in the synagogue on the first day the Torah is read after a daughter's birth. This honor is called *aliyah latorah* עֲלִיָּה לַתּוֹרָה, "going up to the Torah." The baby girl's name is mentioned in a special blessing.

In more recent times, Reform and some Conservative Jews have developed the ritual of naming a baby girl into a more formal one, for which both parents bring their daughter to the synagogue to be named. This custom usually takes place thirty days after the birth. As awareness of sexual equality grows, many Jews have felt the need to create even more significant ways of celebrating the arrival of baby girls into the Jewish community. While there is yet no standard, universal ritual for celebrating the joining of the Jewish community by baby girls, families increasingly perform a ceremony created by the Reform movement. The ceremony is called *Berit Bat*, the "Covenant of a Daughter." (Similar ceremonies called *Berit Hachayim* בְּרִית הָחַיִּים, "Covenant of Life," and *Simchat Bat* שִׂמְחַת בַּת, "Rejoicing in a Daughter," are performed to welcome little girls into the community.) *Berit Bat* ceremonies officially welcome female infants into the Jewish community and into the ancient *berit*, the covenant between God and the Jewish people.

There is no set time for performing a *Berit Bat* or other rituals of welcome for a daughter. Those who want to parallel the *Berit Bat* with the *Berit Milah* celebrate the *Berit Bat* on the eighth day of a baby girl's life. Others generally celebrate within the first thirty days of a daughter's life.

Customs of the Berit Ceremony

Candlelighting at a Berit Milah.

The ceremonies for *Berit Milah* and *Berit Bat* are very simple, but additions can be made to increase their beauty and the joy they create. The room may be decorated with flowers and balloons. A special *Kiddush* cup may be used, and people may dress up for this important occasion. By embellishing these ceremonies, we are enhancing the *mitzvah* of welcoming a new member into our community. Preparing and using attractive objects for a Jewish ritual or working to add to the beauty of a *mitzvah* is called *hiddur mitzvah* הִדּוּר מִצְוָה, "enhancing a *mitzvah*."

Candles are customarily lit at the start of a *berit* ceremony, particularly at a *Berit Bat*. The light of the candle symbolizes the concept of the Jewish people as a "light unto the nations" (Isaiah 42:6), making the world a better place by living good lives as Jews. Lighting the candles expresses the wish for the baby to grow up to perform deeds that will bring light to the world.

During the ceremony the child may be placed on a special blanket or cloth. The blanket used for a child's *berit* ceremony can later be embroidered with blessings and symbols significant to the child. It may then be sewn into a special Torah binder called a wimple. This wimple is used to bind the Torah at the child's bar or bat mitzvah and other important times in his or her life when he or she is called to the Torah. Using a particular blanket during the *berit* ceremony or making a wimple for later use is another example of *hiddur mitzvah*.

A wimple, Germany, sixteenth century.

The Berit Ceremony

Preparations for a circumcision.

The actual *berit* ceremony begins when the baby is brought into the room. The *kvatterin* (Yiddish for "godmother") takes the baby from the mother and gives it to the *kvatter* (Yiddish for "godfather"), who brings the child into the room where the ceremony is to take place. Everyone present stands and recites a Hebrew blessing. This blessing welcomes the infant and the prophet Elijah, who is considered the forerunner of the Messianic Age, the messenger of the covenant, and a protector of little children (Malachi 3:23-24). Then the parents say a prayer in which they accept responsibility for bringing the baby into the covenant shared by the Jewish people.

If the ceremony is a *Berit Milah*, the *kvatter* now hands the baby to the *mohel* or *mohelet*, who places the infant on a special chair set aside in honor of the prophet Elijah. The *mohel* or *mohelet* then lifts the baby from the Chair of Elijah and places him on a pillow on the lap of the *sandak* סַנְדָּק, the person who holds the infant during the circumcision. *Sandak* comes from the Greek work *synteknos*, which means the "helper of the child." While the *sandak* holds the baby, the *mohel* or *mohelet* performs the circumcision and says a prayer thanking God for giving us the ritual of circumcision. Then the parents recite a blessing. If the ceremony is a *Berit Bat*, a rabbi performs the ceremony, and prayers similar to those recited at a *Berit Milah* are said without mentioning circumcision.

The baby's parents choose close relatives or friends to be the *kvatterin*, the *kvatter*, and the *sandak*. Sometimes the parents may select other people as godparents, who gently pass the baby from one to another. Being a child's godparent or *sandak* is considered a very great honor. It is the parents' way of saying that the one they have chosen is someone they cherish, and they hope their child will grow to cherish that person, too.

The *mohel* or *mohelet* or the rabbi then chants the *Kiddush* קִדּוּשׁ, the blessing over wine, and puts a drop of wine into the baby's mouth. Then he or she recites a special prayer wishing the baby a life of Torah study and good deeds and a happy lifelong marriage. The baby's Hebrew name is announced as part of this prayer. Some families then devote a few minutes to explaining why they have chosen a particular name for their child. If a special naming certificate or *berit* certificate has been prepared, they may read it to the guests.

The *Shehecheyanu*, a blessing recited on special occasions, is said as part of the *berit* ceremony. Guests may join the *mohel* or *mohelet* or rabbi in singing or saying this blessing.

The ceremony ends with the *Birkat Kohanim* בִּרְכַּת כֹּהֲנִים, a blessing from Numbers (6:24-26), the fourth book of the Torah. This simple but beautiful prayer asks for God's blessing and for God to watch over and grant peace to the baby. The people in the room participate in this blessing by saying "May this be God's will" in response to each line of the blessing and by saying "Amen" at the end. After this blessing someone holds up the baby for everyone to see, and all the guests happily say "*Mazal Tov* מַזָּל טוֹב."

We enhance happy occasions and holidays by sharing a festive meal called a *seudat mitzvah* סְעֻדַּת מִצְוָה. After a *berit* ceremony, guests join the family in the *seudat mitzvah*. Before this meal, as with all meals where bread is eaten, we recite *Hamotzi* הַמּוֹצִיא, the blessing over bread. (Because this is a festive meal, we usually serve challah חַלָּה.) It is also tradi-

tional to conclude a *seudat mitzvah* with *Birkat Hamazon* בִּרְכַּת הַמָּזוֹן, a blessing that thanks God for the food we have eaten.

To welcome the baby, friends and family at a *Berit Milah* will say, *Baruch haba* בָּרוּךְ הַבָּא, "Blessed is he who comes," or *Beruchah haba'ah* בְּרוּכָה הַבָּאָה, "Blessed is she who comes." Then the *Berit Milah* begins. In addition to *Kiddush*, *Hamotzi*, and *Shehecheyanu*, there are several prayers specifically said for a *Berit Milah*.

Just before the circumcision, the following blessing is said by the *mohel* or *mohelet*:

בָּרוּךְ אַתָּה, יְיָ אֱלֹהֵינוּ, מֶלֶךְ הָעוֹלָם, אֲשֶׁר קִדְּשָׁנוּ בְּמִצְוֹתָיו וְצִוָּנוּ עַל הַמִּילָה.

We praise You, Adonai our God, Ruler of the universe, who sanctifies us with Your commandments and commands us concerning circumcision.

Immediately after the circumcision, one or both parents say the following blessing:

בָּרוּךְ אַתָּה, יְיָ אֱלֹהֵינוּ, מֶלֶךְ הָעוֹלָם, אֲשֶׁר קִדְּשָׁנוּ בְּמִצְוֹתָיו וְצִוָּנוּ לְהַכְנִיסוֹ בִּבְרִיתוֹ שֶׁל אַבְרָהָם אָבִינוּ.

We praise You, Adonai our God, Ruler of the universe, who sanctifies us with Your commandments and commands us to bring our son into the covenant of Abraham, our father.

After one or both parents say the blessing, all the guests say the following:

כְּשֵׁם שֶׁנִּכְנַס לַבְּרִית, כֵּן יִכָּנֵס לַתּוֹרָה וּלְחֻפָּה וּלְמַעֲשִׂים טוֹבִים.

As he has entered into the covenant, so may he attain the blessings of Torah, marriage, and a life of good deeds.

After the *mohel* or *mohelet* or the rabbi says *Kiddush* and announces the child's Hebrew name, one of them blesses the baby with the following words:

יְבָרֶכְךָ יְיָ וְיִשְׁמְרֶךָ. יָאֵר יְיָ פָּנָיו אֵלֶיךָ וִיחֻנֶּךָּ. יִשָּׂא יְיָ פָּנָיו אֵלֶיךָ וְיָשֵׂם לְךָ שָׁלוֹם.

May God bless you and watch over you. May God show you favor and be gracious to you. May God show you kindness and grant you peace.

The ceremony is then concluded with *Hamotzi*.

Pidyon Haben– Redemption of the Firstborn

We have just learned about the ceremonies in which Jewish children are welcomed into the Jewish community and into the ancient covenant between God and the Jewish people. *Pidyon Haben* פִּדְיוֹן הַבֵּן is a different type of ceremony because it is not performed for every Jewish infant. It is reserved for a male infant who is his mother's firstborn child. *Pidyon Haben* is an ancient ceremony, rooted in the Torah (Exodus 13:13 and Numbers 18:15,16). During a *Pidyon Haben* ceremony, parents "redeem" or "buy back" the first son, who was traditionally obligated to work in the Temple. This ceremony is now rarely performed by Reform Jews because it conflicts with the desire to treat Jewish boys and girls equally.

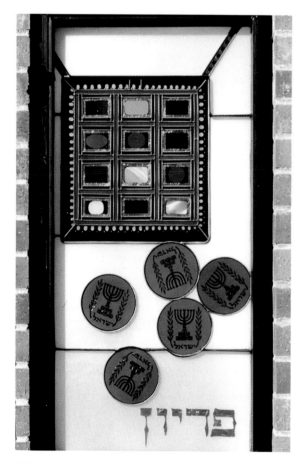

This Plachte-Zuieback art glass window celebrates Pidyon Haben.

Conversion– Another Way of Joining the Jewish Community

Not everyone in the Jewish community is born Jewish. An adopted child enters the community through the *berit* ceremonies described above. The *mohel* or *mohelet* includes a blessing mentioning that the child was not born Jewish but is entering into the community as a Jew on that day. These actions serve as the child's conversion. It is traditional to take a baby boy or girl who is at least six months old to the *mikveh* מִקְוֶה for a ritual immersion. During this simple but moving ritual, one of the parents takes the baby into the *mikveh*, an oversized bathtub with steps leading into it. The baby is very briefly immersed in the water.

For parents of an adopted child, both the *berit* ceremony and the *mikveh* are especially wonderful events, for they mark the long-awaited addition of a new member to the family. They also fulfill the parents' much-anticipated desire to add a new member to the Jewish community.

More common, however, is adult conversion. For various reasons, there are non-Jewish adults who choose to become Jews. The Hebrew term for a convert is *ger* גֵּר. (A female convert is a *giyoret* גִּיוֹרֶת.) In recent years, the significance of this move has resulted in the phrase "Jews-by-choice." The most important requirement for conversion is an in-depth study of the Jewish religion: ritual, practice, Bible, Hebrew language, history, and philosophy. This study may be pursued in a formal conversion class or with a private tutor.

The two other steps traditionally required are circumcision for a male convert and immersion in the *mikveh* for both men and women. Although circumcision and *mikveh* are not universally required by Reform rabbis, study is. Some rabbis suggest a formal public ceremony to mark a convert's entry into the Jewish community. The ceremonial path a convert takes to enter the Jewish community is cause for celebration for both the convert and the community. According to Judaism, a converted individual must be treated as one who has been Jewish all his or her life.

Mikveh, *Johann C. Müller, Germany, eighteenth century, engraving, printed in black. Photography by Lelo Carter.*

The Story of Ruth

A fierce drought forced Elimelech of the tribe of Judah to move his wife, Naomi, and their two sons to the land of Moab. The two sons married Moabite women, but both the sons and Elimelech died in Moab, leaving Naomi and her two daughters-in-law widows. When Naomi decided to return to Bethlehem, one of the daughters-in-law, Ruth, insisted on going with her. Ruth said, "Your people shall be my people, and your God, my God."

The barley harvest was beginning, and being poor and a widow, Ruth gleaned for stalks of grain. By luck, the field was owned by Boaz, a relative of Naomi. In ancient Israel, the law decreed that if a man died childless, as Ruth's husband had, his widow was obligated to marry one of his relatives and name the first child after the deceased.

Naomi was pleased that Ruth had been gleaning in Boaz's fields, for she knew him to be a good man. At the end of the harvest, Ruth and Boaz were married. They had a son named Obed, who became the father of Jesse, who was the father of David, the king of Israel.

SUMMARY

There are several ways in which children are welcomed into the Jewish community. Although *Berit Milah* rituals were originally intended only for boys, today *Berit Bat* rituals for girls welcome girls equally into the Jewish community.

Non-Jews who convert to Judaism must also be welcomed as new members of the community. Adults who convert must participate in a serious course of Jewish study. Once a conversion ceremony has been completed, the participating individual is considered a Jew and, according to Maimonides, may no longer be referred to as a "convert."

To fulfill their roles as members of the community, all Jews must learn about Judaism. For children this education begins at an early age. In the next chapter we will explore the importance of Jewish education as a lifelong pursuit.

As Sweet As Honey

Once upon a time, there was a man named Simcha the Shoemaker. If someone in Simcha's town needed help, only a word to Simcha was necessary. He was such a good and generous man that even the angels in heaven knew of his kind acts.

Simcha lived in a small house with his wife and their son, Matok. Although Matok was only three, everyone could see that he was exceptionally intelligent. Matok knew the names of all the flowers in the field. He could tell you when it was going to rain and when it would be a nice day.

Everyone was sure that Matok would be a great scholar when he grew up. Everyone, that is, except Simcha.

Simcha knew that although Matok was very smart, he was also very lazy. Day after day, Simcha would try to interest Matok in learning the alphabet or in memorizing a few simple prayers. But Matok would always say, "Oh, father, the sky is so beautiful! Please let me look at it a little longer."

The only way Simcha could get Matok to do anything was to give him a bit of something sweet to eat. Then Matok would willingly do anything that Simcha

asked. But there were few sweet things to eat in that little house. The pennies that Simcha brought home each day were used to buy basic foods like flour, salt, and potatoes. There was no room in the budget for expensive "extras" like sugar or candy.

When Matok was four, Simcha told him it was time to begin his religious education so he could learn to read the Bible and pray properly in *shul*. Of course, Matok was not enthusiastic about going to school.

He wasn't sure what school would be like, and he was a little afraid of leaving the comfort of his home. He preferred staying near his house, gazing at the sky and enjoying all God's creation.

The night before Matok was to start school, Simcha stayed up all night and worried. How could he lessen Matok's fears and encourage him to look forward to learning in school?

Simcha's concern for Matok moved the angels, and they began to talk to one another. "Simcha is such a good man," they said. "How can we help him and his son?"

They talked and talked. Finally one angel said, "Matok likes things that are very sweet. And that makes sense since his name, Matok, means sweet. So, let's gather the sweetest honey from the very best hives, and I'll show you what we can do."

Working together, the angels gathered the honey, and while it was still dark, they put a drop of honey on the top and bottom of each page of Matok's schoolbook.

The next morning, when Matok opened his book in class, he noticed something sticky on the top of the page. He rubbed it and licked it with his finger. It was honey! Not only was it honey, but it was the very sweetest honey he had ever tasted. He let his eyes scan the whole page and travel to the bottom of the page. There he saw another dot. He touched it, and it, too, was sticky. Again he licked his finger and found more of the most delicious honey in the whole world. Matok began to think, "Gee, maybe school isn't so bad after all!" He soon came to appreciate the sweetness of learning even without being enticed by honey.

When he grew up, Matok became a famous teacher. Parents brought their children from miles away to his school because they heard that he knew how to transmit the sweetness of learning to children.

Do you know how he did it? On the first day of school, Matok put honey on the pages of each new student's book. The students would read and lick the honey off each page. Soon they would discover that learning is "as sweet as honey." This technique for teaching young children was so successful that it soon became a custom in many Jewish communities around the world. In fact, there are places where this tradition continues to this very day.

ADAPTED FROM SIDRAH STORIES, STEVEN M. ROSMAN, UAHC PRESS, 1989

The Torah— Where Jewish Learning Begins

In Proverbs 3:18 we read, "The Torah is a tree of life to all who hold fast to it." By this we mean that the Torah contains all the knowledge one needs to lead a good life. By studying (holding fast to the) Torah, we learn how to live lives filled with sweetness, joy, and satisfaction. The Torah also binds the Jewish people together. Jews may differ on the details of how to pray or celebrate a particular holi-day, but we all feel connected to the Torah because we place it at the center of our Jewish lives.

Understanding the Torah is a lifelong activity. When we're young, we understand some things but not others. As we mature, those things that didn't make sense to us become clearer, and even what we did understand takes on a deeper meaning. That is why there is no end to Torah study. The Torah is not like a book that you put down and never touch again after reading the last page. Every Shabbat morning we read a section of the Torah in the synagogue. By following a pattern of reading the entire Torah within an annual cycle, we read the Torah from beginning to end year after year, and we do not stop after reading the last page. When we have finished the last line of Deuteronomy, the fifth and final book of the Torah, we immediately begin reading the first line of Genesis, the first book of the Torah.

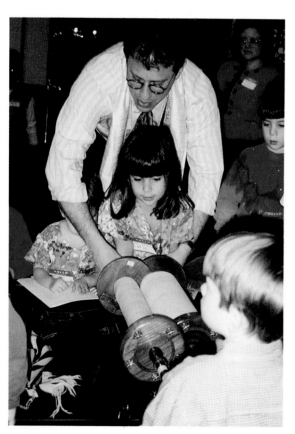

Before You Begin Your Formal Jewish Education

Ideally, Jewish education begins at home. In many households, children learn by watching their parents perform Jewish tasks: lighting and blessing candles on

Friday night for Shabbat שַׁבָּת, setting the table for Friday night dinner, and

A religious school teacher shows students a dreidel.

reciting the blessings over the wine and challah. In some homes, families work together to build and decorate a *sukah* סֻכָּה for the holiday of Sukot סֻכּוֹת. In many others, families say the blessings and light the candles on the eight nights of Chanukah. Many families work together to prepare the Pesach פֶּסַח seder סֵדֶר, the Passover dinner service. Therefore, even before a child starts a formal Jewish education, the beginnings of a Jewish education are taking root at home. By now you have advanced far enough in your Jewish education to have learned many things about the Jewish holidays and the ritual objects and observances associated with them.

TEXT STUDY

At the Passover seder, we are commanded by God to teach the story of the Jewish people's departure from Egypt. For many Jewish children, the Passover seder is an ideal environment to learn about their heritage and history.

When, in time to come, your son asks you, "What mean the exhortations, laws, and rules that *Adonai* our God has enjoined upon you?" you shall say to your son, "We were slaves to Pharaoh in Egypt, and *Adonai* freed us from Egypt with a mighty hand. *Adonai* wrought before our eyes marvelous and destructive signs and portents in Egypt, against Pharaoh and all his household; and us God freed from there, that God might take us and give us the land that had been promised on oath to our ancestors. Then *Adonai* commanded us to observe all these laws, to revere *Adonai* our God, for our lasting good and for our survival, as is now the case. It will be therefore to our merit before *Adonai* our God to observe faithfully this whole Instruction, as God has commanded us.

DEUTERONOMY 6:20-25

The Jewish View of Education

Education has always been a high priority among Jews. At a time in history when education was restricted to the wealthy, Judaism supported the idea that all men, regardless of wealth or social status, had to be educated so they could study Torah. Jews studied Hebrew and sacred Jewish texts. Over the years, some secular studies like science and mathematics were added to the list of subjects they studied.

Today we continue to place a high value on education by sending young boys *and* girls to Jewish religious schools, where they learn to read Hebrew, gain an understanding of their Jewish heritage, and prepare to become educated members of the Jewish community.

The First Step to Your Jewish Education

As we said earlier, under the best circumstances, religious education should start in the home as early as possible. As your parents teach you how to eat at the table or speak respectfully to others, so should a Jewish education begin at home. If a parent was not born Jewish or did not receive a Jewish education, that parent may need help to learn what is required to be a good Jewish educator for his or her children. Fortunately, today many books and teachers are available to assist such parents.

While it's important to learn about Judaism at home, religious school provides students with the added benefit of allowing them to share their Jewish educational

A religious school Shabbat Shalom *project.*

experience with other young Jews. At the same time that parents may have enrolled their children in nursery school to prepare them for secular school, they may also have taken their children to a synagogue nursery program to help them get a feeling for Jewish learning and Jewish activities. Some synagogues even have Jewish parenting programs for parents of children too young for nursery school.

Entering Religious School

Religious schools select different grades to mark the beginning of their pupils' education. Some start as early as kindergarten and first grade; others wait until their students reach the second or third grade. To mark this important step in religious education, many schools celebrate with a special synagogue ceremony called consecration. The word *consecration* means to "make sacred."

The concept of a consecration ceremony—setting aside time to mark the beginning of a Jewish child's formal religious education—is derived from several Jewish customs: One popular custom was for a parent to send the child to school with cookies baked in the shape of Hebrew letters, thus helping the child learn the Hebrew alphabet. Another custom was to write the Hebrew letters in honey on the child's slate. Both these customs emphasize the sweetness of education.

Hillel on the Roof

So famous were the reputations of the Torah teachers Shemayah and Avtalyon that Hillel walked all the way from Babylonia to Jerusalem to study with them. Hillel's desire to learn from these scholars was so great that he went to work to pay for his studies.

One Friday, Hillel could not find any work. Unable to pay the watchman of the house of study, he climbed to the roof and listened through the skylight to that day's lesson. So intent was Hillel on the lesson that he didn't notice it had begun to snow.

The next day, the two Torah scholars walked into the study house and noticed that their room was darker than usual. When they looked up at the skylight, they saw a strange sight: Hillel lay unmoving on the roof, his body covered with snow. The two scholars brought the freezing student down from the roof and into the house and rubbed him with warm towels. Just as they were about to build a fire, they remembered the Sabbath rule forbidding them to do so. But Avtalyon said, "To save a life, we are permitted to break even the law of the Sabbath."

"Truly," Shemayah replied. "This man deserves to have the law of the Sabbath broken on his behalf."

So the teachers built the fire, and Avtalyon said, "His love of learning must be great. It is certain that one day this Hillel will become a distinguished sage in Israel."

The Consecration Ceremony

A consecration ceremony at a small town synagogue.

Consecration ceremonies are usually held in the synagogue on Simchat Torah שִׂמְחַת תּוֹרָה, the joyous holiday on which we celebrate the end of one cycle of Torah reading and the beginning of a new cycle. Simchat Torah means the "Joy of the Torah." On Simchat Torah, the Torah scrolls of the congregation are carried by a procession of people, singing and dancing. These processions are called *hakafot* הַקָּפוֹת. In some congregations, as a reminder of the sweetness of Torah study and Jewish learning, children are given candy as the Torahs are carried around the sanctuary. Other congregations serve candy and sweet fruit after the services.

Simchat Torah is a logical choice for consecration ceremonies because both Simchat Torah and consecration mark beginnings. Simchat Torah is the day on which we finish and then begin again the cycle of Torah readings. A consecration ceremony marks the beginning of a young person's formal Jewish education.

The way in which synagogues celebrate consecration varies greatly. Some congregations hold consecration ceremonies only for children entering kindergarten or first grade. Other synagogues consecrate students of all ages who are entering religious school for the first time.

There is no one "right way" to plan a consecration. Some congregations celebrate consecration with great ceremony. Others incorporate it into the regular synagogue calendar. In congregations where young children are consecrated in a formal way, the children may wear white robes and carry white flowers or candles as they walk from the back of the sanctuary to the *bimah* בִּימָה.

In almost all consecration ceremonies, the children's participation is an important aspect of the event. In most cases, the consecration class has learned certain prayers and songs for this occasion. Individually or as a group, they may recite the *Barechu* בָּרְכוּ, the *Shema* שְׁמַע, the short *Kiddush*, and *Hamotzi* at the appropriate times in the service. Sometimes they sing as well.

Typically, congregations will give a gift to consecrants during the service. Some congregations present the students with a special consecration certificate, their own prayer book or other special book for their Jewish bookshelf, or their own miniature Torah. If a child does not yet have a Hebrew name, a naming ritual may also be included as part of the consecration service.

In many congregations, the rabbi blesses the consecrants. Usually the children are called up to the *bimah* for this honor, and as the ark is opened, the congregation rises. Rabbis most frequently bless the consecrants with *Birkat Kohanim*, the "Priestly Blessing" (Numbers 6:24-26). However, some rabbis use other blessings as well and may even write their own.

Because of the significance we place on education, much of which is centered around studying and understanding the Torah and all books of Jewish learning, Jews are called the "people of the Book."

This consecration ceremony on Simchat Torah welcomes new religious school students.

Among the first things Jewish children learn upon entering religious school are certain prayers central to Jewish life. Three of the most common are the *Shema, Kiddush,* and *Hamotzi.*

Shema

שְׁמַע יִשְׂרָאֵל: יְיָ אֱלֹהֵינוּ, יְיָ אֶחָד.

Hear, O Israel: Adonai is our God, Adonai is One.

Kiddush

בָּרוּךְ אַתָּה, יְיָ אֱלֹהֵינוּ, מֶלֶךְ הָעוֹלָם, בּוֹרֵא פְּרִי הַגָּפֶן.

We praise You, Adonai our God, Ruler of the universe, Creator of the fruit of the vine.

Hamotzi

בָּרוּךְ אַתָּה, יְיָ אֱלֹהֵינוּ, מֶלֶךְ הָעוֹלָם, הַמּוֹצִיא לֶחֶם מִן הָאָרֶץ.

We praise You, Adonai our God, Ruler of the universe, for causing bread to come forth from the earth.

SUMMARY

In this chapter we have seen that the Torah is a source of continuing life for the Jewish people. For thousands of years we have drawn strength from it, and it has helped us lead good lives even in difficult times.

When you enter religious school and are consecrated, you are beginning your journey on the road to formal Jewish education—a journey that will continue throughout your life. In additon to learning in formal classes, you will also learn by reading, listening to records, watching movies, and talking to people who will share their Jewish life experiences with you, e.g., in a youth group or at a Jewish camp. Thus, Jewish education will not be limited to religious school. There are opportunities for Jewish learning all around you. You must take the time to notice and take advantage of them.

In the next chapter we shall see how Jewish education prepares you for the first steps toward Jewish adulthood.

Two Tales of Becoming Bar Mitzvah

Many years ago, in a small town, there lived a wealthy tax collector and his family. When it was time for the man's son to become bar mitzvah, the tax collector invited all the important people in the area to the feast. This was to be the most costly and extravagant party ever given in the history of the town.

On the morning of the celebration, the tax collector discovered that the Ba'al Shem Tov, a great and learned man who was the founder of Chasidism, was visiting the town. The tax collector went to see the Ba'al Shem Tov and begged him to attend his son's bar mitzvah feast.

At first, the Ba'al Shem Tov was reluctant to accept the invitation because he was visiting the town to minister to the poor. The tax collector was so insistent, however, that the Ba'al Shem

Tov finally agreed to attend.

In those days, it was customary to invite the poorest people of the town to attend a bar mitzvah or a wedding feast. The tax collector, however, did not do this because he thought, "Why should my important guests have to share a table with beggars dressed in rags?"

The great day arrived, and all the guests assembled. At the head of the table, next to the bar mitzvah, sat the great Ba'al Shem Tov. He rose to say a few words of greeting and then stopped. Suddenly he chuckled, and then he laughed out loud. The great Ba'al Shem Tov then started to make sounds like barnyard animals: He mooed like a cow, neighed like a horse, clucked like a

chicken, and quacked like a duck.

The guests couldn't believe their eyes and ears. Suddenly they were all laughing until the tears streamed down their faces.

Finally the laughter subsided, and the Ba'al Shem Tov, wiping the tears from his eyes, said, "My dear friends, let me explain what has just happened.

"As I rose to speak, I had a vision of a tiny farm far away. A young orphan boy lives there, and he, too, became bar mitzvah today. Before the boy's father died, he told his son that on his thirteenth birthday he would be called up to the Torah in the synagogue, and everyone would say Amen to his blessing.

"Well, the farm is so isolated that there's no congregation nearby. So today, the boy went into the barnyard and spoke to his only companions: his horse, his cow, and his duck. He said, 'Today I become bar mitzvah. If we were in a town, I would be called to the Torah and be blessed, and the *minyan* would say Amen. But since we are here on the farm, you must be my *minyan*.'

"Then the boy said, 'Ruler of the universe, I give thanks for my life, for the companions surrounding me, and for Your bringing me to this wonderful day when I gladly take responsibility for performing Your commandments.'

"Then each of the animals said Amen in its own way. The cow mooed, and I mooed with the cow. The duck quacked,

and I quacked with the duck. The horse neighed, and I neighed with the horse.

"The angels were watching, and when the animals said Amen, the angels began to laugh. And when angels laugh, all the world laughs. And that's why I laughed, and that's why you laughed."

The rich man stood up with tears in his eyes, but these were not tears of laughter. "Dear guests," he said, "I thought I could bring blessing upon my son by surrounding him with the best material things the world has to offer. But now I understand that blessing comes not from what a person has but from what is in a person's heart. And I am ashamed that my heart has been so selfish."

Then his son said, "Father, let's invite all the poor people of the village to this feast, and let's find the young orphaned boy and bring him here, too."

The father praised his son for his compassion and did all that his son had suggested. He raised the orphaned boy as his own son. The two boys grew up together and studied together, and everything they did brought honor and joy to their community.

FROM A STORY SUGGESTED BY
STEVEN M. ROSMAN

How Bar and Bat Mitzvah Developed

Becoming bar or bat mitzvah, a "son or daughter of the commandment," is a life-cycle stage—like becoming a teenager—that you enter at the age of thirteen. You become bar or bat mitzvah whether or not you are called to the Torah, whether or not you have a ceremony in the synagogue, or whether or not you have a party.

We learned about the words *ben* בֵּן and *bat* בַּת, "son of" and "daughter of," when we talked about naming. The word *bar* בַּר is the Aramaic equivalent of the Hebrew word *ben*. We use the Aramaic term because at the time the concept of a bar mitzvah ceremony was developing, Aramaic was the prevalent language of the Jews. The bat mitzvah ceremony was developed in the twentieth century by non-Orthodox Jews in North America, who chose to use the Hebrew word *bat* because Hebrew is the language now used during services.

Most cultures have ceremonies that mark puberty, the onset of adulthood. According to most scholars, the idea that Jewish adulthood begins at age thirteen developed during the Second Temple period in Israel (516 B.C.E. to 70 C.E.). During this period, a father brought his thirteen-year-old son to the Temple in Jerusalem to receive a blessing.

An actual ceremony celebrating Jewish adulthood began to develop sometime during the sixth century C.E. However, it was not until the thirteenth or fourteenth century that the custom of calling a thirteen-year-old boy up to the Torah was firmly established.

In the twentieth century, as attitudes toward women changed, a ceremony was developed to mark twelve- or thirteen-year-old girls' entry into the adult Jewish community, too. The first known bat mitzvah in North America was held in 1922 for Judith Kaplan, whose father, Rabbi Mordecai Kaplan, was the founder of the Reconstructionist movement. This innovation found favor with the Reform movement and developed quickly into the format we use today.

A triplet bat mitzvah, ca. 1940.

The First Bat Mitzvah

Judith Kaplan Eisenstein

At the time of my twelfth birthday, the age at which Jewish law recognizes a girl as a woman, subject to the *mitzvot*, "commandments," there had been no synagogue where such a ceremony could be conducted.

It would be less than the whole truth to say that I was as full of enthusiasm about the subject of the ceremony as my father was. I was worried about the attitude of my own peers— the early teenagers who even then could be remarkably cruel and disapprove of the "exception," the person who does not conform to the normal practice.

On the Shabbat morning of my bat mitzvah, we all went together—father, mother, disapproving grandmothers, my three little sisters, and I—to the brownstone building on 86th Street where the Society carried out all its functions.

Women's rights or no women's rights—the old habit of separating the sexes at worship died hard. The first part of my own ordeal was to sit in that front room among the men, away from the cozy protection of mother and sisters.

The service proceeded as usual, through *Shacharit*, the "Morning Service," and through the Torah reading. Father was called up for the honor of reading the *Maftir*, the last section of the Torah reading.

When we finished the *haftarah*, a reading from the Prophets, I was signaled to step forward to a place below the *bimah* at a very respectable distance from the scroll of the Torah, which had already been rolled up and garbed in its mantle. I pronounced the first blessing and from my own *Chumash*, the Five Books of Moses, read the selection that my father had chosen for me, continued with the reading of the English translation, and concluded with the closing *berachah*, "blessing." That was it. The scroll was returned to the ark with song and procession, and the service resumed. No thunder sounded, and no lightning struck. The institution of bat mitzvah had been born without incident, and the rest of the day was all rejoicing.

ADAPTED FROM AN ARTICLE IN *KEEPING POSTED*, VOL. XXVII, NO. 3, JANUARY 1982

Why Becoming Bar or Bat Mitzvah Is Important

The Jews are an ancient people with a history that dates back over 5,000 years. This is one of many ways in which we differ from other religious communities existing today. Every Jew is a link in this continuous 5,000-year-old chain. Each time we celebrate bar or bat mitzvah, we are welcoming a new adult into the Jewish community and a new link in the chain.

When you celebrate becoming bar or bat mitzvah, you are stating that you want to be counted as one of our people, as one of the links in the chain of an ancient tradition. You are saying you want to add your efforts to strengthening this 5,000-year-old chain by studying Torah and learning the *mitzvot* מִצְווֹת. You are publicly demonstrating that our people is very much alive and well. That's why becoming bar or bat mitzvah is important. In fact, many adults who did not have a bar or bat mitzvah ceremony and celebration at thirteen choose to have one.

A bat mitzvah, draped in her talit, *reads from the Torah.*

One who becomes bar or bat mitzvah demonstrates devotion to Jewish study by learning to read, chant, and even interpret Torah and *haftarah* portions. This love of and respect for learning is emphasized repeatedly in *Pirke Avot*.

Hillel and Shammai received [the Tradition] from them. Hillel said, "Be one of Aaron's students, loving peace and pursuing it, loving people and bringing them to the Torah."

Pirke Avot 1:12

He [Hillel] used to say, "If I am not for

myself, who will be for me? And if I am for myself alone, then what am I? And if not now, when?"

PIRKE AVOT 1:14

Shammai said, "Make your Torah [study] a habit; say little, but do much; and greet every person cheerfully."

PIRKE AVOT 1:15

FOCUS

The Bar or Bat Mitzvah Ceremony

Although each synagogue has its own customs, almost all Reform bar and bat mitzvah ceremonies include at least two of the following elements:

1. Reading the appropriate Torah portion and reciting the appropriate *berachot* בְּרָכוֹת, "blessings," related to the performance of this *mitzvah*. The honor of being called up to the Torah is called an *aliyah* עֲלִיָּה.

2. Reading the appropriate *haftarah* הַפְטָרָה (a selected portion from the Prophets) and reciting the appropriate *berachot*. It is traditional to *chant* the cantillated Torah and *haftarah* portions and their blessings. While some Reform synagogues follow this practice, others allow the bar or bat mitzvah to *read* the Torah and *haftarah* portions.

3. In addition to the Torah and *haftarah* readings, the bar or bat mitzvah celebrant may also lead part of the service and give a brief speech.

Although almost all bar or bat mitzvah services follow this outline, students with special needs can have a bar or bat mitzvah ceremony tailored to their abilities. The important factor is that the student makes an effort to master some kind of Jewish learning.

Usually a bar or bat mitzvah ceremony takes place on a Saturday morning close to the young person's thirteenth birthday.

The Bar-Mitsvah, *Moritz Oppenheim, painting, Germany, nineteenth century.*

Some congregations also include participation in the Shabbat service on the preceding Friday night. Other possible times for the ceremony are Friday night; Saturday afternoon; and Monday, Thursday, and festival mornings. These are all times when we read the Torah.

LIFE-CYCLE BLESSINGS

An appropriate blessing for a bar or bat mitzvah is the **Birkat Kohanim**.

יְבָרֶכְךָ יְיָ וְיִשְׁמְרֶךָ. יָאֵר יְיָ פָּנָיו אֵלֶיךָ וִיחֻנֶּךָּ. יִשָּׂא יְיָ פָּנָיו אֵלֶיךָ וְיָשֵׂם לְךָ שָׁלוֹם.

May God bless you and watch over you. May God show you favor and be gracious to you. May God show you kindness and grant you peace.

The bar or bat mitzvah also learns the blessings said before and after reading the Torah.

Before reading the Torah
Reader:

בָּרְכוּ אֶת־יְיָ הַמְבֹרָךְ!

Congregation:

בָּרוּךְ יְיָ הַמְבֹרָךְ לְעוֹלָם וָעֶד!

Reader:

בָּרוּךְ אַתָּה, יְיָ אֱלֹהֵינוּ, מֶלֶךְ הָעוֹלָם, אֲשֶׁר בָּחַר־בָּנוּ מִכָּל־

הָעַמִּים וְנָתַן־לָנוּ אֶת־תּוֹרָתוֹ. בָּרוּךְ אַתָּה, יְיָ, נוֹתֵן הַתּוֹרָה.

Reader: *Praise Adonai, to whom our praise is due!*

Congregation: *Praised be Adonai, to whom our praise is due, now and for ever!*

Reader: *Praised is Adonai our God, Ruler of the universe, who has chosen us from all peoples by giving us the Torah. We praise You, Adonai, Giver of the Torah.*

After reading the Torah

בָּרוּךְ אַתָּה, יְיָ אֱלֹהֵינוּ, מֶלֶךְ הָעוֹלָם, אֲשֶׁר נָתַן לָנוּ תּוֹרַת אֱמֶת וְחַיֵּי עוֹלָם נָטַע בְּתוֹכֵנוּ. בָּרוּךְ אַתָּה, יְיָ, נוֹתֵן הַתּוֹרָה.

Praised is Adonai our God, Ruler of the universe, who has given us a Torah of truth, implanting within us eternal life. We praise You, Adonai, Giver of the Torah.

Ways to Enhance the Bar and Bat Mitzvah Experience

Twinning This is a program in which you "adopt" a Jewish child from a country where religious discrimination against Jews has prevented that child from having a bar or bat mitzvah ceremony. You will receive information about the child and he or she will be symbolically called to the Torah with you on the day of your bar or bat mitzvah ceremony.

Tzedakah Donate a sum of money to a worthy cause that you have researched

A father holding a talit *made for his son's bar mitzvah.*

and have decided to support.

Talit Ceremony In congregations where a *talit* is worn by the bar and bat mitzvah celebrants: Before your *aliyah*, your parents or other relations may present you with a *talit*—either a new one or one that has been handed down in your family. Put on the *talit* and say the appropriate blessing.

Heirloom Ceremony Your parents or other relatives may present you with a family heirloom such as a *Kiddush* cup or *talit* and explain its meaning. If the rabbi agrees, this can be included in the bar or bat mitzvah service. This can also be included at a celebration after the service.

Family Tree In the year leading up to your bar or bat mitzvah, work with your family to develop a detailed family tree. Display it at the synagogue or party and distribute it to other family members.

Bar or Bat Mitzvah Project For a period of time before your bar or bat mitzvah, study a subject of Jewish interest or participate in a social action program, such as working in a soup kitchen or tutoring underprivileged children. Use what you have studied or experienced in the program as the theme of your bar or bat mitzvah *devar Torah*.

The Celebration

Elaborate bar or bat mitzvah parties are not new. Since the thirteenth century, rabbis have been concerned that sometimes the party gets more attention than the religious ceremony.

Of course, there is nothing wrong with having a party to celebrate this momentous step in your Jewish life cycle. In fact, the idea of celebrating a religious event with a party is very much a part of Judaism. This kind of party is called a *seudat mitzvah*, a festive meal that accompanies the performance of a *mitzvah*. As we saw in an earlier chapter, the *seudat mitzvah* is also part of a *Berit Milah* or *Berit Bat* ceremony.

Traditionally, a *seudat mitzvah* would immediately follow the bar or bat mitzvah ceremony. Thus many parties today are luncheons. However, some families choose to have a *Kiddush*, consisting of a light snack, for the congregation at the synagogue after the Saturday morning service and then have a dinner party in the evening.

Regardless of the type of party you and your parents choose, remember that the party is the celebration of a religious life-cycle event, marking a significant achievement in a young person's religious life. Here are some suggestions for bringing that message into the party:

- Before anyone eats or drinks at the party, the new bar or bat mitzvah should lead the guests in reciting the *Kiddush*, the blessing over wine or grape juice, and *Hamotzi*, the blessing over bread. Make copies of these prayers in Hebrew and in transliteration so everyone can participate.
- At the end of the meal, have the bar or bat mitzvah, a close relative, or an honored guest lead everyone in the *Birkat Hamazon*, the prayer of thanksgiving after meals.
- Have someone teach Israeli folk dancing during the party. Although this is not a religious activity, it is a way of showing your conscious identification with Israel and the Jewish people.

It is traditional for the bar or bat mitzvah to lead Kiddush.

- Instead of flower arrangements, make the table centerpieces from a stack of new Jewish books, with a note that they will be donated to your synagogue library or classrooms.
- At each table, place a printed card explaining that a sum of money equivalent to a percentage of the bar or bat mitzvah celebration expense is being donated to a Jewish organization, e.g., the organization called Mazon, which addresses hunger concerns.

Life after Bar and Bat Mitzvah

Bar or bat mitzvah is not the end but rather the beginning of serious Jewish study. Successful preparation for bar or bat mitzvah means the student will be able to read Hebrew with some fluency and understand basic Jewish concepts, including the meaning of performing *mitzvot*.

Lifelong study is one of the most important *mitzvot* in Judaism. After becoming bar or bat mitzvah, the young person has the obligation to fulfill this *mitzvah*. This can be done by continuing in the synagogue's confirmation program or enrolling in a Hebrew high school program.

SUMMARY

We have learned in this chapter that becoming bar or bat mitzvah is an important step in the Jewish life cycle. It is a change marked by a religious ceremony whereby you announce to the world that you are ready to be a full member of the Jewish community, an ancient group of people whose traditions and teachings have survived over 5,000 years.

Although the ceremony is not strictly necessary to become bar or bat mitzvah, it is an important part of your confirming your Jewish identity. As you continue your education, the feeling of belonging to the Jewish people will deepen and grow.

In the next chapter we will look at what happens after one becomes bar or bat mitzvah and how we carry out the important Jewish value of continued learning.

The Inheritance

Once upon a time, many years ago, there was a wealthy Jewish woman who had only one daughter. On the evening before her daughter's marriage, the woman came into her daughter's bedroom holding a small felt bag in her hand. She took her daughter's hand and, opening the mouth of the bag, let the contents of the bag fall into her daughter's palm.

The daughter looked down and gasped in amazement. It was a perfectly formed opal about the size of a chicken's egg. There was something about the jewel that made her feel it was alive. It felt warm in her hand, and it flashed with all the colors of the rainbow.

The mother closed her daughter's fingers around the jewel and said to her, "This jewel is beyond price. It is the only one of its kind in the world. On the evening of my wedding, my mother gave this opal to me. Now I pass this inheritance on to you.

"The more you hold this jewel and admire it, the more beautiful it will become. However, because it's so valuable, be sure to keep it in this bag and put it in a safe place."

The daughter married and had a daughter of her own. She often took the opal from its bag, cradling it in her hands and admiring its fiery beauty. When her own daughter was about to get married, she gave her daughter the opal, saying, "This is a valuable jewel that has been passed down by the women in our family from generation to generation. Keep it in this bag and put it in a safe place." The woman forgot to tell her daughter about the importance of handling the opal, and she did not put the jewel in her daughter's hand. Instead, she opened the mouth of the bag and had her daughter look at the jewel inside the bag. She

thought this would make the jewel seem even more precious.

Generation after generation of daughters became mothers and presented the opal to their daughters on their wedding night. The mothers all stressed the great value of the jewel, but the information about holding and admiring it was lost. In fact, it became customary to not even open the bag. It seemed to the women that keeping the jewel hidden made it even more special and precious.

After many years, one of the women in this family found herself in desperate financial trouble. Her dearly loved young husband had died of a terrible disease. All their money was gone, and she was left alone in the world with six young children and no means of supporting them. They were about to lose their home; there was no food in the house; and there was no money with which to buy any.

The only possession of any value this woman owned was the opal. She had never seen the jewel, but she knew that the bag given to her by her mother on the evening before her wedding held something of enormous value. If she could sell it, her financial troubles would be over.

In her humble home, there was no safe, but the woman had hidden the bag in a hole in the dirt floor beneath her bed.

She could barely move the bed to get to the place where the bag was hidden. She pushed and shoved for what seemed like hours. Finally, drained by exhaustion and with shaking hands, she found the hiding place and uncovered the bag.

The knots were hard to open, and she worked and worked to pry them loose. As she did this, visions of a warm home with a table set with hot food for herself and her children danced before her eyes. The future looked bright again, and her heart was filled with hope. With trembling fingers, she opened the bag and held it upside down so the jewel would fall into her lap.

Shimmering dust trickled out of the opening and made a small mound on her skirt. She shook the bag, thinking that perhaps the jewel had become stuck in the lining, but nothing more came out. She peered into the bag but saw nothing. She put her hand inside, searching frantically, but the bag was empty. Where was the opal?

Opals are a special kind of jewel. They must be handled; they must be cared for. Without the warmth of human hands and the oils of human skin, opals lose their fire, become brittle, and turn to dust.

Confirmation— A New Jewish Life-Cycle Ceremony

Confirmation is about claiming our Jewish inheritance. When you become bar or bat mitzvah, you have mastered certain Jewish "basics": reading Hebrew, learning some prayers, some understanding of the Jewish life cycle, knowledge of the Jewish festivals, and familiarity with the Bible. However, these basics are just the beginning of your Jewish education.

Confirmation is a relatively new Jewish life-cycle ceremony, dating back to the early 1800s. The first confirmation ceremonies were substituted for bar mitzvah ceremonies and were organized like graduation exercises. In 1822, a class of thirteen-year-old boys *and* girls were confirmed at the Reform synagogue in Berlin. Eventually bar mitzvah (and later bat mitzvah) ceremonies came back into popular Reform practice, and confirmation was postponed until a later stage in a student's religious education, between ninth and twelfth grades. Since then, confirmation has been firmly linked to advanced Jewish learning.

Early in the development of confirmation as a life-cycle celebration, it was linked to Shavuot שָׁבוּעוֹת, the holiday that celebrates the giving of the Torah to the Jewish people and their acceptance of it. The revelation of the Torah and its acceptance by the Jewish people presented an excellent framework for the confirmation ceremony. At the confirmation ceremony, young men and women who are now mature enough to make their own decisions publicly reaffirm their Judaism and their roles as full members of the Jewish community.

Confirmation ceremonies are held on Shavuot, the holiday that celebrates the giving of the Torah to the Jewish people.

The decision made by the confirmands means that they will behave as responsible Jewish adults, following the laws of the Torah that were handed to Moses at Mount Sinai. The most important laws are those found in the Ten Commandments.

The Ten Commandments

1. I am *Adonai* your God, who brought you out of the land of Egypt.
2. You shall have no other gods beside Me. You shall not make idols of anything in the sky, on the land, or in the water. You shall not bow down to them or serve them.
3. You shall not swear falsely by the name of God.
4. Remember the Sabbath and keep it holy.
5. Honor your father and your mother.
6. You shall not murder.
7. You shall not commit adultery.
8. You shall not steal.
9. You shall not testify falsely under oath.
10. You shall not covet.

Confirmation Celebrations Today

From the early twentieth century to the years around World War II, confirmation was an extremely important life-cycle ritual for young Jewish men and women. We know from photos that many synagogues located in metropolitan areas had very large confirmation classes. In these photos, the confirmands are dressed very formally. The young women are usually wearing long white dresses, and the young men are in dark suits and ties. The women often hold white bouquets, and the *bimah* is lavishly decorated with white floral arrangements. At that time, confirmation ceremonies were generally held when confirmands reached the age of sixteen.

One of the reasons confirmation was

An early confirmation class, ca. 1880.

63

seen as so important was because the bar mitzvah ceremony did not then receive the emphasis it is given today. In addition, most Reform synagogues did not encourage bat mitzvah ceremonies for women. The focus of a young person's Reform Jewish education was confirmation, and it was this ceremony, usually celebrated in conjunction with Shavuot, that marked the major life-cycle event for Jewish teenagers.

The actual Shavuot/confirmation service often incorporated Hebrew and English readings from the Torah and the Prophets, presented by the confirmands. Sometimes members of the confirmation class led parts of the service or the entire service. Individuals also made speeches or presented interpretations of the biblical readings.

The tone of the confirmation ceremony changed somewhat during the mid-1960s and early 1970s. In keeping with the spirit of the times, many synagogues did away with the formal white dresses and dark suits. The floral displays in the synagogue became less elaborate. Shavuot, however, continued to be a focus for the ceremony.

The actual service also began to change. Though readings from the Torah and the Prophets, speeches, and original interpretations of the Torah portion remained the main part of the service, new songs and readings from sources other than the prayer book found their way into the ceremony.

Today the confirmation age and type of ritual vary from synagogue to synagogue. However, almost all Reform synagogues celebrate confirmation on or around Shavuot. In some synagogues, the ceremony is held privately with the rabbi and members of the confirmation class. In other communities, a more formal atmosphere surrounds the ceremony. In such cases, the members of the class often wear white robes and prepare and lead a special service designed for the occasion. Often a celebratory dinner for family and students precedes the service. Some congregations have linked completion of confirmation with a class trip to Israel.

A confirmation class, Temple Israel of Detroit, 1969.

Confirmation—Claiming Your Inheritance

The word *confirmation* denotes conscious acknowledgment. When we speak of confirmation as indicated by the Jewish ceremony of confirmation, we are referring to a ritual in which post-bar and bat mitzvah young men and women clearly reaffirm the responsibilities of Jewish adulthood they have taken upon themselves as full members of the Jewish community.

While this may sound like "Bar or Bat Mitzvah, part II," there is a very important difference. Your becoming bar or bat mitzvah is often a decision your parents have made with you. Confirmation, the commitment to continue your Jewish education, is your own adult decision. By participating in a confirmation class and the culminating ceremony, you are making a public statement of your ties to the Jewish people and Judaism.

Most synagogues have a special curriculum to prepare students for confirmation. Although curricula differ from synagogue to synagogue, they often include study

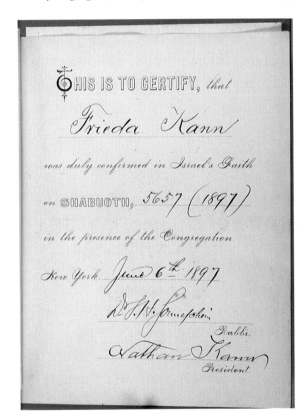

This 1897 confirmation certificate with its seal (left photo) is an example of the kind of certificate received by confirmands.

about Israel and the history of the Jewish people; student participation in *gemilut chasadim* גְּמִילוּת חֲסָדִים, "acts of loving-kindness," either individually or as a class; and discussions about God, Jewish rituals, Torah study, and Jewish culture.

Why Continue Your Jewish Education after Bar or Bat Mitzvah?

As we learned in the chapter "Entering Religious School," the *mitzvah* of Jewish education is a lifelong undertaking. Surely you would never end your secular education at the age of thirteen. Why conclude your Jewish education after bar or bat mitzvah at the age of thirteen? You would be deprived of much wonderful learning, and much of your Jewish heritage would go unclaimed.

Because of your growing maturity and understanding in the years between celebrating bar or bat mitzvah and confirmation, you will begin to explore your Jewish heritage more deeply. Questions will arise that you did not think about while preparing for your bar or bat mitzvah ceremony. Studying for confirmation will give you several additional years to investigate new ideas and understand Judaism and Jewish customs in deeper, more meaningful ways.

Consider Jewish education as progress through different stages of personal transportation: During your early years of Jewish learning, you are riding a tricycle. At consecration, the beginning of your formal Jewish education, you advance to a two-wheeler with training wheels attached. When you become bar or bat mitzvah, you are whizzing around on a mountain bike. By confirmation, you are no longer riding a bike but learning to drive a car. Wouldn't it be a pity if you had never advanced from a tricycle to a two-wheeler? Or if you didn't take off the training wheels? Or if you never learned to drive a car? Just as there is more to learn about and concentrate on driving a car, there is more to learn about the Jewish past and Jewish living today. By reaching confirmation, you have gained a great deal of knowledge and proved you can continue learning on your own.

Why You Have to Confirm Your Connection to Judaism

According to Jewish law codes, one who is born a Jew or who converts to Judaism is not required to "prove" his or her Jewish status. However, we also have an ancient tradition in which great Jewish leaders like Moses and Esther were called upon to confirm their connection with the Jewish people through specific actions. Moses had grown up in the Egyptian palace, but as an adult he had to go before Pharaoh and confirm that as the leader of the Jews, he was demanding their freedom from slavery. Esther's confirmation of her Jewish identity also involved going before a king—the king of Persia, her husband, Ahasuerus—and pleading for the lives of her people, who were about to be killed by Haman, the king's evil adviser. Both Moses and Esther had to risk their lives to confirm their connection to the Jewish people. Luckily, your acts of confirmation will not be life-threatening.

Although you are considered a Jewish adult at thirteen, you may still be unsure of the true weight of becoming bar or bat mitzvah. At fifteen or older, you have a much better understanding of the obligations of Jewish adulthood and the importance of being a contributing member of the Jewish community. Confirmation is a ceremony in which you, as a more mature person, reaffirm the commitment to Judaism you made when you were thirteen. Occasionally individuals decide not to celebrate bar or bat mitzvah but, nonetheless, choose to continue their religious education. Generally, confirmation is not restricted to teenagers who have had bar or bat mitzvah ceremonies, but some synagogues have special study requirements for those confirmation students who have not.

Esther before Ahasuerus, *Italy, eighteenth century, engraving after Guercino. Photography by Lelo Carter.*

Life after Confirmation

What you do after confirmation depends on when confirmation takes place in your synagogue. If confirmation takes place at the end of the ninth or tenth grade, your synagogue may have a special high school or youth group program for continuing your Jewish education in both formal and informal settings. If confirmation takes place in the eleventh grade, your synagogue may offer a college preparatory program for your twelfth-grade year. Today many colleges and universities have Jewish Studies courses, and almost all Jewish communities have courses for adults who want to keep up a lifetime of Jewish learning.

SUMMARY

In this chapter we have looked at the importance and meaning of continuing Jewish education after becoming bar or bat mitzvah. Through continuing Jewish education we learn the true value of our Jewish heritage, and we learn to appreciate how living a Jewish life can help us live a happy life.

We have also seen that confirmation is an adult decision. It's something we do for ourselves because we want to be involved adult members of the Jewish community. Attending classes, however, is not the only way to live a Jewish life. In the next two chapters we will explore different ways to continue our Jewish living outside religious school, in our personal lives and our communities.

For Want of a Candle

This story is dedicated to the courageous Jews of Alma-Ata, Kazakhstan, who work every day to maintain their Judaism in the face of anti-Semitism and harsh economic conditions, and to Natasha, the past president of Congregation Shalom.

Once there was a young Jewish girl named Natasha, who lived in a big, beautiful city in northern Russia. Her family loved Judaism. For many years they were happy.

As time passed, however, things began to change. Almost daily, they heard of Jews being beaten or robbed only because they were Jews. One day Natasha's father told the family that the government had decided Jews could no longer live in their town. All the Jews were going to be moved to Alma-Ata, the capital of Kazakhstan, more than 2,000 miles to the south.

Alma-Ata was not a city where Jews had traditionally settled. On the first Friday morning of their new life there, Natasha asked her mother, "Where are we going to get candles, wine, and challah for Shabbat?"

"This week," said Natasha's mother, "we'll do without those things. By next week we'll be able to find all the things we need to make Shabbat the way we did in our old home."

That night, Natasha missed the cheery warmth of the Shabbat candles. The silver *Kiddush* cup gleamed after its weekly polishing, but it was empty. There was no crusty braided challah on the table, only a round, hard loaf of brown bread. It didn't feel like Shabbat.

The next week, Natasha asked her mother, "When will we go to find the things we need for Shabbat?"

70

Her mother answered, "Soon, my dear. As soon as we settle down, we'll begin to look for the things we need. Don't worry. We'll make Shabbat again soon."

A year of Shabbats passed.

One day at school, a new Jewish student, Shlomo, joined Natasha's class. Shlomo and Natasha soon became friends. One day over lunch, Natasha asked him, "What do you miss most about your old home?"

Without even pausing to think, Shlomo answered, " Shabbat. My parents just can't seem to find the things we need to celebrate the way we used to."

"Me, too, " said Natasha. "But what can we do about it? There's no kosher wine, no challah, no candles to buy here."

They sat thinking for several minutes. Then Natasha had an idea. "I saw olive oil in the grocery store," she said. "Maybe if we put a piece of string in a small dish with olive oil, it will burn like a candle."

"I saw grapes in the market, " said Shlomo. "Maybe we could squeeze grapes and make grape juice. After all, the *Kiddush* thanks God for the fruit of the vine, not wine."

"And maybe we could figure out how to make challah!" said Natasha.

Over the next few weeks, Natasha and Shlomo experimented with making grape juice, burning olive oil, and making challah. When they were satisfied with the results, they asked Shlomo's family to

Natasha's home for Shabbat dinner.

When Natasha came home from school that day, she worked to get the house ready for Shabbat. She put a clean white tablecloth on the dining room table, shined the candlesticks that had grown dull from lack of use, and polished the *Kiddush* cup that was badly tarnished. She covered her freshly baked challah with a clean white napkin.

Shlomo brought the olive oil, the wicks, and the grape juice. Together, he and Natasha filled the top of the candlesticks with oil and stuck in the wicks, and they filled the *Kiddish* cup with grape juice. Then they closed the doors to the dining room so no one would see what was inside.

When Natasha's parents and Shlomo's family arrived, Natasha and Shlomo greeted them with smiles and a resounding *Gut Shabbes*. Then they opened the doors of the dining room with a flourish. Natasha said, "Shlomo and I have been longing for Shabbat. We know that it's not easy to get the things we're accustomed to, so we decided to find new ways to celebrate."

Then Natasha lit the wicks in the oil-filled candlesticks and said the blessing welcoming Shabbat. Shlomo raised the *Kiddush* cup filled with grape juice and chanted the *Kiddush*. Then Natasha brought out the challah that she and Shlomo had baked and invited everyone to say *Hamotzi* together.

"Natasha," her father said, tears on his cheeks, "you and Shlomo have reminded us that there is always a way to live our lives as Jews. When we came here, we were confused and unhappy. When we couldn't find something as simple as candles for our Shabbat candlesticks, we gave up. Your creativity has given us Shabbat once again."

Suddenly, everyone was crying tears of joy and hugging one another. Natasha and Shlomo looked at each other and grinned. There were so many things to do! They wanted to make *mezuzot* for the doorposts of their Jewish homes. Chanukah was just around the corner, and they would need *menorot*. The future held so many wonderful possibilities.

JO DAVID

Living a Jewish Life

So far we have looked at some of the milestones in the Jewish life cycle: birth and naming, conversion, entering religious school, becoming bar or bat mitzvah, and being confirmed. However, we know that life is more than a series of landmark events. In the years between entering religious school and being confirmed, and throughout our adult lives, we live through years of experience. You have learned the importance of continuing your Jewish education after religious school and for the rest of your life. In this chapter we will look at many of the ways you can lead a full Jewish life even when you're not preparing for a life-cycle event. There are many opportunities to make Jewish choices.

Jewish Spirituality

For Jews, spirituality means having an ongoing relationship with God. Jewish spirituality means living a life that is influenced by Jewish rituals, ideas, and values. The word for this kind of focus is *kavanah* כַּוָּנָה, "intention."

Thanking God for things we do or experience is one way of remembering our special relationship with God. There are prayers and rituals for almost everything that happens to us in our lives. For example, when you eat a piece of seasonal fruit for the first time, it's traditional to say the *Shehecheyanu*. When you see a rainbow in the sky, there's a special prayer to thank God for that experience.

If you're not accustomed to having prayers and rituals in your daily life, it may seem overwhelming to think about adding so much "Jewish thinking" to the things you do. Many people who want to add more spirituality to their lives begin by saying *Hamotzi* each time they eat a piece of bread. This simple ritual reminds us that the bread we eat comes not only through our own efforts but also through God's kindness to us. Each time we think of God, we add a little more spirituality to our daily existence.

The Jewish Home

What makes a Jewish home different from another home? The most obvious symbol is the *mezuzah* מְזוּזָה affixed to the outside doorpost. The commandment to put up a *mezuzah* comes from the *Shema* (Deuteronomy 6:9), in which we are told to inscribe God's instructions to us on the doorposts of our houses and gates.

In addition to a *mezuzah*, there are other signs that show us we are in a Jewish home. Many families display their Shabbat and holiday ritual objects. For Friday night they may have candlesticks; a *Kiddush* cup; a special challah plate, covered by a challah cover; and even a challah knife. For the Saturday night *Havdalah* הַבְדָּלָה service they may have a special *Kiddush* cup, a braided candle, a special candleholder, and a spice box. A *chanukiah* חֲנֻכִּיָּה (Chanukah *menorah*), a seder plate,

and a *lulav* לוּלָב and *etrog* אֶתְרוֹג are some other holiday ritual objects.

Building a Jewish Library

A very special feature of a Jewish home is its Jewish bookshelf or library. There are many books in print about Jewish subjects from archaeology to zoology. You can continue your Jewish learning after religious school by reading Jewish books and putting them in your own Jewish library. You can set aside one special bookshelf for only Jewish books, and you can continue adding to it throughout your life.

At the heart of any Jewish library should be our most important book, the Torah. The other books of the Bible and a prayer book are also basic building blocks of a Jewish library. A Jewish bookshelf could also contain books on Jewish history and books about Jewish rituals and traditions. Jewish culture has a worldwide literature of folktales, legends, stories, and poetry, as well as music and art.

When you make your Jewish bookshelf, you can also include computer programs and CD-ROMs on Jewish topics. You can easily find many Jewish games and interactive books on CD-ROMs or on the Internet or World Wide Web. To include current events on your Jewish bookshelf, find out if your community has a local Jewish newspaper to which you can subscribe. There are Jewish magazines that publish news and literature. These can also be added to your Jewish bookshelf.

Kashrut— Dietary Codes

A European kosher stamp, used by ritual slaughterers to certify meat as kosher.

You can find more clues that identify a Jewish home by looking in the kitchen. Some Jewish families "keep kosher," that is, they follow the laws of *kashrut* כַּשְׁרוּת. The laws of *kashrut* were developed from statements in the Torah about which foods Jews may or may not eat. One of the best known is "You shall not boil a kid in its mother's milk" (Exodus

23:19, Exodus 34:26, and Deuteronomy 14:21). From this statement, rabbis derived the commandment to keep dairy and meat foods separate. Some Jews implement this commandment by not combining milk and meat in the same dish or at the same meal. Others actually have two separate sets of dishes, silverware, and cooking utensils: one set for meat and one for dairy. *Pareve* is a Yiddish word applied to foods that are considered neither meat nor dairy. Some *pareve* foods are fish, vegetables, fruit, and eggs.

Other passages in the Torah divide animals into two classes: those that are permitted to be eaten and those that are forbidden. The Torah specifically mentions winged insects, small creeping things, fish and other water animals, and different kinds of birds and mammals (Leviticus 11:1-23 and Deuteronomy 14:3-21). Some Jews simply refrain from eating those foods, like pork and shellfish, that are listed in the Torah as forbidden. Other Jews will eat only those foods that are stamped with a kosher seal of approval, which means they have been certified as kosher by a board of rabbis, and some people will eat only in approved restaurants.

Animals that are permitted as food must be slaughtered in the most painless way possible by a butcher who is specially trained. The meat must then be cleaned according to very particular instructions.

People who are concerned with caring for animals and the environment do not eat veal or other meats normally permitted to Jews because they disagree with the way the animals are raised and treated. There are also many Jewish vegetarians, who believe that the best way to keep kosher is by eating no meat. People who practice eco-*kashrut*, which takes its name from the word *ecology*, do not eat fruits and vegetables that have been treated with chemicals and pesticides. They believe using substances harmful to the environment breaks the commandment of *Bal Tashchit* בַּל תַּשְׁחִית, "Do Not Destroy." We will learn more about *Bal Tashchit* later in this chapter.

Hachnasat Orechim– Hospitality

Welcoming guests into our homes is a very important part of Jewish life. This subject is first mentioned in the story in the Torah (Genesis 18:1-8) where Abraham welcomes three strangers into his home with great kindness and consideration for their needs. This story is the foundation for the *mitzvah* of *hachnasat orechim* הַכְנָסַת אוֹרְחִים, "hospitality." When we read the *haggadah* הַגָּדָה on

75

Abraham and the Angels, *Shmuel Bonneh, 1970, oil on canvas. Gift of Mimi and Leon Feldman. Photography by Lelo Carter.*

Pesach, we refer to this *mitzvah* when we say, "All who hunger, let them come and eat; all who are in need, let them come and celebrate the Passover." Inviting guests for Shabbat dinner and festival meals is also considered a very important fulfillment of the *mitzvah* of *hachnasat orechim.*

Gemilut Chasadim— Deeds of Loving- Kindness

A central characteristic of living a Jewish life is performing *gemilut chasadim*, "deeds of loving-kindness." These deeds cover every aspect of life, including visiting the sick, comforting mourners, being kind to a sibling, doing a favor for a friend, donating money to a charity, and doing something in your home without being asked. According to our tradition, we are commanded to perform acts of kindness. We are expected to be God's partners in the work of *tikkun haolam* תִּקּוּן הָעוֹלָם, "repairing the world." We are obligated to perform *gemilut chasadim* without any expectation of reward and with *kavanah*, the "intention" of helping others.

Every year as the High Holy Days approach, we must think about our actions during the past year. Have we always been as kind, honest, and fair as we should have been? If not, we need to show that we're sorry by doing *teshuvah* תְּשׁוּבָה, "repentance." Doing *teshuvah* literally means "turning away" from our bad behavior. We do *teshuvah* by asking those we've hurt for their forgiveness and by

Visiting the elderly is an example of gemilut chasadim, *"acts of loving-kindness."*

working hard performing *gemilut chasadim* to make up for our wrong actions.

Tikkun Haolam–Repairing the World

From its early development, Reform Judaism has been concerned with the concept of social action. Our concern for social action means that we care about and work for the rights and needs of people not only in the Jewish community but in the world around us.

In Hebrew, the special term for social action is *tikkun haolam*, "repairing the world." Working with God to repair the world is the job of every Jew. Sometimes young people feel there is nothing they can do to help repair the world, but, in fact, we all have special talents that God has given us. It's up to us to determine what is wrong in our own communities today and to use our talents to help change the "wrongs" to "rights."

Tzedakah–Helping Those in Need

One of the most important acts in Judaism is giving *tzedakah* צְדָקָה. Although *tzedakah* means "righteousness,"

it is often translated as charity. This is an incomplete translation. We give charity voluntarily, out of kindness and generosity. But *tzedakah* is a *mitzvah*, a "commandment" to help those in need. We must fulfill this *mitzvah* whether or not we feel especially generous or kind. Of course, giving to others out of a good heart is all the better. We usually think of *tzedakah* as giving money to the needy, but it can also include giving food, donating clothing and other goods, and giving of our time to help others.

This Plachte-Zuieback art glass window illustrates the importance Judaism places on the value of justice.

The prophets of the Hebrew Bible often wrote of God's desire for the Children of Israel to do good in the world.

God has told you, O humanity, what is good, and what *Adonai* requires of you: only to do justice, to love goodness, and to walk modestly with your God.

MICAH 6:8

Many Jewish writings discuss the individual's responsibility for giving *tzedakah*.

You shall not close your hand against your needy kinsman.

DEUTERONOMY 15:7

Tzedakah outweighs all other religious precepts.

TALMUD, *BAVA BATRA*

Even a poor man living on *tzedakah* should give *tzedakah*.

TALMUD, *GITTIN*

If you see one giving liberally, it means one's wealth will grow; if you see one who shuns *tzedakah*, it means one's wealth will dwindle.

MIDRASH MISHLE

Who is kind to the poor lends to *Adonai*.

PROVERBS 19:17

Bikkur Cholim— Visiting the Sick

An important way to help others is by performing the *mitzvah* of *bikkur cholim* בִּקוּר חוֹלִים, "visiting the sick." The Talmud teaches that a kind and understanding visitor can help lighten a sick person's burden and even alleviate one sixtieth of a person's suffering (*Nedarim* 39a). Visitors should offer their full attention and loving-kindness, as well as a prayer for healing. The real gift, of course, is the desire just to be with someone who is sick. *Bikkur cholim* is good medicine for the entire community, and by visiting those who are ill, we become more connected to and beloved by our God and community.

Bikkur cholim is a *mitzvah* for every Jew, not only for the rabbi or cantor of a congregation. In the temple, during the prayer for healing, it is a *mitzvah* to say the name of a person who is ill. While a person's English name may be used, it's traditional to give the sick person's Hebrew name and his or her mother's Hebrew name. This stems from the belief that God is more attentive to the cries of mothers for their sick children.

Nachman of Bratslav was a famous chasidic rabbi who expressed many beautiful thoughts. Below is a poem he wrote about our appreciation of nature.

Master of the universe, grant me the
ability to be alone:
May it be my custom to go outdoors
each day
Among the trees and grasses, among all
growing things.
There to be alone and enter into
prayer.
There may I express all that is in my
heart,
Talking to *Adonai* to whom I belong.
And may all grasses, trees, and plants

Awake at my coming.
Send the power of their life into my
prayer,
Making whole my heart and my
speech
Through the life and spirit of growing
things,
Made whole by their transcendent
Source.
O that they would enter into my
prayer!
Then would I fully open my heart
In prayer, supplication, and holy
speech;
Then, O God, would I pour out the
words
Of my heart before Your presence.

Bal Tashchit— Do Not Destroy

Tree-planting shows concern for the environment.

In the Torah we are told that God made the world for our use. We also learn that God put people in the Garden of Eden to tend it (Genesis 2:15). Although we have been given the right to use the wonderful natural resources of the earth for our well-being, we are also commanded to be responsible for the care of these resources. The *mitzvah* of *Bal Tashchit*, "Do Not Destroy," teaches us that we must never willfully destroy any natural resources or commit vandalism on any property, including our own. *Bal Tashchit* is a law of conservation within Judaism.

There are many blessings we say at various times in our lives as Jews: blessings for the home, the dinner table, and nature's wonders. Blessings serve several purposes at once: They acknowledge God's presence in all we see and do; they make seemingly ordinary actions and events holy; they remind us to think about the importance of what we do and see.

One of the blessings we say to help make our home Jewish is the blessing before affixing a *mezuzah*.

בָּרוּךְ אַתָּה, יְיָ אֱלֹהֵינוּ, מֶלֶךְ הָעוֹלָם, אֲשֶׁר קִדְּשָׁנוּ בְּמִצְוֹתָיו וְצִוָּנוּ לִקְבּוֹעַ מְזוּזָה.

Blessed is Adonai our God, Ruler of the universe, by whose mitzvot we are hallowed, who commands us to affix the mezuzah.

We have already learned some of the blessings we say before a meal (e.g., *Kiddush* or *Hamotzi*). Another important blessing is *Birkat Hamazon*, which we say after a meal. Below is part of the prayer.

Birkat Hamazon

Leader:

חֲבֵרַי נְבָרֵךְ.

Response:

יְהִי שֵׁם יְיָ מְבֹרָךְ מֵעַתָּה וְעַד עוֹלָם.

Leader:

יְהִי שֵׁם יְיָ מְבֹרָךְ מֵעַתָּה וְעַד עוֹלָם. בִּרְשׁוּת חֲבֵרַי נְבָרֵךְ (אֱלֹהֵינוּ)* שֶׁאָכַלְנוּ מִשֶּׁלּוֹ.

Response:

בָּרוּךְ (אֱלֹהֵינוּ)* שֶׁאָכַלְנוּ מִשֶּׁלּוֹ וּבְטוּבוֹ חָיִינוּ.

Leader:

בָּרוּךְ (אֱלֹהֵינוּ)* שֶׁאָכַלְנוּ מִשֶּׁלּוֹ וּבְטוּבוֹ חָיִינוּ. בָּרוּךְ הוּא וּבָרוּךְ שְׁמוֹ.

Together:

בָּרוּךְ אַתָּה יְיָ אֱלֹהֵינוּ מֶלֶךְ הָעוֹלָם הַזָּן אֶת־הָעוֹלָם כֻּלּוֹ בְּטוּבוֹ בְּחֵן בְּחֶסֶד וּבְרַחֲמִים. הוּא נוֹתֵן לֶחֶם לְכָל־בָּשָׂר כִּי לְעוֹלָם חַסְדּוֹ. וּבְטוּבוֹ הַגָּדוֹל תָּמִיד לֹא חָסַר לָנוּ וְאַל יֶחְסַר לָנוּ מָזוֹן לְעוֹלָם וָעֶד בַּעֲבוּר שְׁמוֹ הַגָּדוֹל. כִּי הוּא אֵל זָן וּמְפַרְנֵס לַכֹּל וּמֵטִיב לַכֹּל וּמֵכִין מָזוֹן לְכָל־בְּרִיּוֹתָיו אֲשֶׁר בָּרָא. בָּרוּךְ אַתָּה יְיָ הַזָּן אֶת־הַכֹּל.

* Said when ten or more are present at the meal.

וּבְנֵה יְרוּשָׁלַיִם עִיר הַקֹּדֶשׁ
בִּמְהֵרָה בְיָמֵינוּ. בָּרוּךְ אַתָּה יְיָ
בּוֹנֵה בְּרַחֲמָיו יְרוּשָׁלָיִם. אָמֵן.

Leader: *Friends, let us say grace.*

Response: *May God's name be blessed now and for ever.*

Leader: *May God's name be blessed now and for ever. Let us bless our God of whose bounty we have partaken.*

Response: *Blessed be our God of whose bounty we have partaken and through whose goodness we live.*

Leader: *Blessed be our God of whose bounty we have partaken and through whose goodness we live. Blessed be God and blessed be God's name.*

Together: *Blessed are You, Adonai our God, Ruler of the universe, who sustains the whole world with goodness, with grace, with kindness, and with tender mercy. God gives food to every creature, for God's kindness endures for ever. Through God's great goodness, food has never failed us, and may it not fail us for ever and ever, for God's great name's sake. For God nourishes and sustains all and does good unto all, providing food for all the creatures whom God has fashioned. Blessed are You, Adonai, who gives food to all.*

And build Jerusalem as a holy city speedily in our time. Blessed are You, Adonai, who in mercy builds Jerusalem.

Some other blessings express our appreciation and awe of nature's wonders.

On seeing lightning or other natural wonders

בָּרוּךְ אַתָּה, יְיָ אֱלֹהֵינוּ, מֶלֶךְ
הָעוֹלָם, עֹשֶׂה מַעֲשֵׂה בְרֵאשִׁית.

Blessed is Adonai our God, Ruler of the universe, the Source of creative power.

On hearing thunder

בָּרוּךְ אַתָּה, יְיָ אֱלֹהֵינוּ, מֶלֶךְ
הָעוֹלָם, שֶׁכֹּחוֹ וּגְבוּרָתוֹ מָלֵא
עוֹלָם.

Blessed is Adonai our God, Ruler of the universe, whose power and might pervade the world.

On seeing a rainbow

בָּרוּךְ אַתָּה, יְיָ אֱלֹהֵינוּ, מֶלֶךְ
הָעוֹלָם, זוֹכֵר הַבְּרִית וְנֶאֱמָן
בִּבְרִיתוֹ וְקַיָּם בְּמַאֲמָרוֹ.

Adonai our God, Ruler of the universe, You are the Blessed One. You keep faith with us, and, true to Your word, You remember Your covenant with creation.

Finding a Jewish Community

From their earliest days in America, Jews have organized and supported community groups that have satisfied a wide range of needs. Some of these groups were private businesses; others were welfare and cultural organizations. One way to continue living a Jewish life after confirmation is by volunteering your time to one of these organizations. Not only will you be performing the work of *tikkun haolam*, but you will also become an important member of your Jewish community.

Another way to become a more active member of the Jewish community is to join a local synagogue or *chavurah* חֲבוּרָה. When you leave your parents' home to go away to school or set up your own home, joining a synagogue or another Jewish group is an excellent way to feel comfortable in a new city. For college students, there are usually several opportunities for Jewish affiliation: a Hillel or KESHER (the Reform movement's college outreach program) group, a student *chavurah*, or a local synagogue that welcomes college students.

A Jewish basketball team, ca. 1920.

Israel

From the earliest days of history, Israel has been the center of Jewish hopes and dreams. However, people of religions other than Judaism also consider Israel their ancestral homeland. Like the United States, Israel promises freedom to all religions.

Jews growing up in America can strengthen their connection to Israel by learning about Israel's history and culture and by following the news about issues affecting Israel today. In this way, we can better understand Israel's place in our history as a people and our place in Israel's existence as a modern state.

Traveling to Israel is a special experience

for Jews living in the Diaspora. There are programs available for those who want to visit Israel to study, to volunteer on a kibbutz, to explore nature, or to travel. Israel is the land of the Bible. While we can read about places like Tiberias, Beersheva, and Jerusalem in the Bible, today we can visit those cities and walk the same ground that Abraham, Isaac, Rachel, and Jonah did years ago. Israel is a living laboratory for learning about and understanding the Bible and our historical roots.

There are many ways to provide Israel with political, financial, and cultural support. Groups like ARZA (the American Reform Zionist Association) and WZO (the World Zionist Organization) are dedicated to supporting Israel as a Jewish state and a homeland for all Jews. By joining or donating to these organizations, we can support different kinds of projects related to Israel.

Some Jews feel such a strong connection to the Jewish state that they make *aliyah* to Israel. After almost two thousand years, the reality of a Jewish homeland is a miracle. A Jew living anywhere in the world has the right to immigrate to Israel and become an Israeli citizen.

The poem "Hatikvah" הַתִּקְוָה, written by Jewish poet Naphtali Herz Imber (ca. 1878), beautifully expresses the Jewish longing for a homeland in Zion. It was adopted as the Israeli national anthem.

כָּל עוֹד בַּלֵּבָב פְּנִימָה
נֶפֶשׁ יְהוּדִי הוֹמִיָּה,
וּלְפַאֲתֵי מִזְרָח קָדִימָה
עַיִן לְצִיּוֹן צוֹפִיָּה.
עוֹד לֹא אָבְדָה תִקְוָתֵנוּ,
הַתִּקְוָה שְׁנוֹת אַלְפַּיִם,
לִהְיוֹת עַם חָפְשִׁי בְּאַרְצֵנוּ,
בְּאֶרֶץ צִיּוֹן וִירוּשָׁלַיִם.

As long as deep in the heart
The soul of a Jew yearns,
And toward the East
An eye looks to Zion.
Our hope is not yet lost,
The hope of two thousand years,
To be a free people in our land,
The land of Zion and Jerusalem.

SUMMARY

In this chapter we have seen different ways in which we can live as Jews. Continuing to learn about Judaism, making a Jewish home for ourselves, reading books, becoming involved in our communities, being concerned about social action and conservation, establishing an important connection with Israel, and leading lives dedicated to making the world a better place for others—all these help us live rich Jewish lives and express pride in our Jewish identity.

CHAPTER EIGHT

JEWISH MARRIAGE

Definitely in Heaven

Once upon a time, in a land far away, there lived a king who believed he could do anything. Since he owned all the land in his kingdom, he could give large plots of good land to peasants and make them rich. He could take away the castles of noblemen and make them poor. With a royal decree, the king could free prisoners or throw free people into dungeons.

In this land, there was a small community of Jews. Their leader was a very wise woman named Malka. She spent her days teaching Jewish children about Judaism, visiting the sick, and helping the poor. She was known far and wide for her kindness and wisdom.

The king knew there were Jews living in his kingdom, but he didn't know anything about them. One day he decided to summon Malka to the palace so he could learn about

the Jews of the community and their beliefs.

Malka and the king spent many hours talking about Judaism. Malka explained that God had made the world in just six days and had rested on the seventh. The king listened very respectfully. Then he asked, "How many years has it been since your God created the world?"

"Many, many years," replied Malka.

"I don't understand," said the king. "It's been many years since the creation of the world. What has your God been doing since then?"

"God has been arranging marriages," responded Malka.

"Arranging marriages!" laughed the king. "I can arrange marriages. It's true I've never thought of doing it, but why shouldn't I? I can do anything I want to do. I'm the king. If all your God does is arrange marriages, then if I arrange marriages, you should worship me instead of your God. Tomorrow I shall arrange a hundred marriages. And at the end of the week, I will expect all the Jews in the kingdom to come to the palace and worship me as their God."

Malka was horrified and quickly left the palace to bring the bad news to the Jewish community.

The next day, the king brought together a hundred young couples and declared them married.

A day passed. And another. It was almost the end of the week when the king's messenger banged excitedly on Malka's door.

"You must come at once," said the messenger. "The king needs you."

Malka hurried to the palace. On her way, she noticed that something was very wrong in the kingdom. Men and women were shouting and crying in the streets.

As she entered the throne room, she saw the king, who looked as though he hadn't slept in several days. There were dark circles under his eyes and a bruise on his cheek.

"Malka, Malka," cried the king. "It's a disaster, a complete disaster!" The king looked as if he were going to cry. "I made a hundred marriages," he said, "and it's been chaos ever since. All the couples are fighting. Everyone's upset. Someone actually threw a ripe tomato at me. I had to cancel all the marriages just to restore some order to the kingdom.

"I thought I could make marriages like your God. Now I understand that making a marriage is no easy task. Truly, it is a task only God should undertake. I'm only a king. Go back to the Jews and tell them they can worship their marriage-making God in peace."

And all lived happily ever after.

BASED ON A RABBINIC LEGEND

Jewish Dating and Jewish Marriage

In ancient times, Jewish marriages were arranged by families, sometimes with the help of a *shadchan* שַׁדְכָן, a "matchmaker." Love was not the primary consideration although it was hoped that a good match would be made and that the husband and wife would grow to love each other. Today, in America, young men and women usually get to know one another before they marry.

Many things attract us to other people. Having similar interests and a similar religious background help us feel comfortable with others. Although it is generally believed that we don't meet those we will marry until we're in our twenties or older, many people begin to date in their early teens.

While it's important to have friends from different religious and ethnic backgrounds, there's something special about Jewish dating. Some Jewish teenagers find it difficult to connect with others of the same religious background. But, within the Jewish community, there are many ways in which teenagers and young adults can meet one another and form friendships—both romantic and nonromantic—that may last a lifetime.

Many teenagers participate in organizations like NFTY (the North American Federation of Temple Youth) and USY (United Synagogue Youth), which run programs for Jewish teenagers all over the

world. Jewish summer camps and leadership institutes also provide a fun-filled, relaxed setting for meeting new people. Hillel and KESHER offer young adults ways to make new friends. Having a circle of Jewish friends increases the likelihood that you will date and eventually marry someone who shares your Jewish values.

Marriage is a sacred act that is deeply rooted in Jewish history. The betrothals and marriages of our matriarchs and patriarchs comprise some of the most beautiful stories in the Torah.

In the Book of Genesis, we read how the servant sent by Abraham to find Isaac a wife brought back the kind and generous Rebecca.

Isaac had just come back from the vicinity of Beer-lahai-roi, for he was settled in the region of the Negeb. And Isaac went out walking in the field toward evening and, looking up, he saw camels approaching. Raising her eyes, Rebecca saw Isaac. She alighted from the camel and said to the servant, "Who is that man walking in the field toward us?" And the servant said, "That is my master." So she took her veil and covered herself. The servant told Isaac all the things that he had done. Isaac then brought her into the tent of his mother Sarah, and he took Rebecca as his wife. Isaac loved her and thus found comfort after his mother's death.

GENESIS 24: 62-67

Isaac's son Jacob has an experience very different from that of his father when he goes to work for his uncle, Laban, in Haran. Jacob is tricked into marrying Leah. Because of what happened to Jacob, we have the Jewish custom of *badeken di kalah*, "inspecting the bride," before the marriage ceremony begins.

Now Laban had two daughters; the name of the older one was Leah, and the name of the younger was Rachel. Leah had weak eyes; Rachel was shapely and beautiful. Jacob loved Rachel; so Jacob said to Laban, "I will serve you seven years for your younger daughter Rachel." Laban said, "Better that I give her to you than that I should give her to an outsider. Stay with me." So Jacob served seven years for Rachel, and they seemed to him but a few days because of his love for her.

Then Jacob said to Laban, "Give me my wife, for my time is fulfilled...." And Laban gathered all the people of the place and made a feast. When evening came, Laban took his daughter Leah and brought her to Jacob....When morning came, there was Leah! So Jacob said to Laban, "What is this you have done to me? I was in your service for Rachel. Why did you deceive me?" Laban said, "It is not the practice in our place to marry off the younger before the older. Wait until the bridal week of this one is over, and we will give you Rachel too, provided you serve me another seven years."

GENESIS 29:16-27

Jewish Marriage Is Holy

In Jewish tradition, God is responsible for making good marriages. When we say a marriage was "made in heaven," it means we believe God was responsible for bringing the couple together. Tradition also teaches that when two Jews marry, God is present at the wedding, helping to get them off to a good start.

Jewish marriage has a special word all its own: *kiddushin* קִדּוּשִׁין. The word *kid-*

While tending Laban's flocks, Jacob sees Rachel.

dushin is related to other Hebrew words you may know: *Kiddush* קִדּוּשׁ, the prayer we say over wine; *kadosh* קָדוֹשׁ, which literally means "holy" and is a word we use to describe God in our prayers; and *Kaddish* קָדִישׁ, a prayer praising God. The words *kiddushin, kiddush, kadosh,* and *kaddish* all have meanings related to a special kind of holiness. In English, we sometimes use the word *sanctified* to describe something we consider holy or something we use only for a very special purpose.

We use the word *kiddushin* for Jewish marriage for several reasons. When we marry, we are telling the rest of the world we are making a holy or sacred commitment to another person. We also believe that celebrating our relationship with our partner in a Jewish ceremony, setting up a Jewish home, and raising Jewish children are all holy acts, leading to the performance of *mitzvot*. Using the word *kiddushin* to describe Jewish marriage underscores the holiness of marriage in Jewish tradition.

According to traditional Jewish law, the term *kiddushin* is applied only to a marriage between a Jewish bride and a Jewish groom. This does not mean that unions between other couples are not holy. They are just not traditional Jewish marriages. Some rabbis help couples where one partner is non-Jewish create ceremonies that use symbols and customs from the traditional Jewish wedding.

The Key Components of a Jewish Marriage Ceremony

- Both parties are Jews who are free to marry according to Jewish law.

- The marriage is conducted by a qualified person in the presence of a *minyan*.

- A *ketubah*, the Jewish "marriage contract," is read and signed by two qualified witnesses called *eidim*. One witness is an *eid*. To qualify as a witness for a wedding performed by a Reform rabbi, a man or woman must be a Jewish adult, not related to either the bride or groom.

- The bride and groom exchange rings and recite vows or promises of commitment.

Jewish Wedding Customs

A Jewish wedding can be performed in any suitable place that is convenient for the bride and groom. Today many couples choose to be married in a synagogue and have a reception afterwards in that synagogue, in a catering hall, a restaurant, or at home.

One of the main features of a Jewish wedding is the *chupah* חֻפָּה. A *chupah* resembles a portable tent with four poles. The *chupah*, the wedding canopy, was originally a piece of velvet or a *talit* attached to four poles. Four male friends or relatives were given the honor of holding these poles.

Today a *chupah* can be very simple or very elaborate. Many couples still choose

Chupa, *Peter Krasnow, 1907, drawing, pencil. Photography by Lelo Carter.*

to use a *talit*. They may purchase a new *talit* for the occasion or use one that has been passed down in the family. Often the *talit* used for the *chupah* is later presented to the couple's child when he or she becomes bar or bat mitzvah. Some couples have a *chupah* designed especially for them. After the wedding, they use the fabric as a wall hanging in their home.

The *chupah* frame may be made of any sturdy material, usually metal or wood. For a more elaborate *chupah*, leaves and flowers may be wrapped around the poles. Whether simply or intricately decorated, the *chupah* serves as a fitting symbol of the home the couple will create together.

Jewish weddings may be performed any day of the week except Shabbat and almost all year long except for certain des- ignated Jewish holidays, fast days, or days of personal mourning.

My Grandmother's Hands–The Wedding, *artist Lynne Feldman, 1990.*

Jewish Marriages Are Not Usually Performed on…

- Shabbat.

- Rosh Hashanah, Yom Kippur, Sukot, Passover, Shavuot. (It is permitted to marry on Purim and Chanukah because these holidays did not originate in biblical times.)

- traditionally, the days between Passover and Shavuot.

- Tishah Be'av and other fast days.

- days when people are in mourning for a close relative.

Before the Wedding

People about to get married are excited and perhaps a little nervous when the wedding day arrives. The *chatan* חָתָן, "groom," the *kalah* כַּלָּה, "bride," and their friends and family gather at the place where the wedding will be held. The rabbi, the groom, the bride (if she wishes), and two witnesses meet to sign the *ketubah* כְּתֻבָּה, the Jewish "marriage contract."

The drawing up and signing of a *ketubah* is an ancient Jewish custom. Archaeologists have discovered *ketubot* כְּתֻבּוֹת that date back to 500 B.C.E. Originally a *ketubah* was a contract by which a man acquired a wife. In ancient times, women were thought of as only daughters or wives, not as independent individuals. While a contract for a wife now sounds objectionable, the *ketubah* was actually meant to protect women and guarantee their rights within and after marriage. It gave women status and protection in the event of a husband's death or in the case of divorce. The *ketubah* described the type of property both the man and woman were bringing into the marriage and guaranteed the wife a certain amount of

money if her husband died before she did or if he divorced her. The *ketubah* was the property of the woman only, not of the couple. If it was lost or destroyed, the couple could not live together until a new *ketubah* was written.

In countries where Jewish communities flourished, beautiful, original *ketubot* illustrated especially for the bride and groom were created. Thus, in many cases, an important legal document also became a work of art. This custom has gained acceptance around the world, and there are those who earn a living as *ketubah* artists.

In ancient times, the text of each *ketubah* was different, but over the years a "standard" text, written in Aramaic, was developed. Today a traditional *ketubah* text or a more modern Jewish wedding document is almost always included as part of a Jewish wedding. While many couples still use the standard Aramaic text, it is now possible to find *ketubot* with different texts in virtually any language. Some couples even write their own *ketubah* text. Most couples preserve their *ketubah* by framing and hanging it within their home.

Before the marriage ceremony begins, some couples take part in a custom called *badeken di kalah*. In this ceremony, the groom comes to where the bride is waiting, looks at her, and then covers her face with

A modern ketubah, *designed by Neil Yerman.*

her veil. Recall the biblical story of Jacob, who worked for seven years to marry Rachel and found that Laban had tricked him by substituting her older sister, Leah. To be certain he is marrying the woman of his choice, the groom himself covers the face of the bride before meeting her under the *chupah*. After *badeken*, the bride and groom proceed to the *chupah*. The groom, escorted by his parents, goes first. The bride, escorted by her parents, follows.

The Marriage Ceremony: Betrothal

From under the *chupah*, the rabbi greets the bride, the groom, and the gathered guests with welcoming words from the Book of Psalms and with traditional blessings. Some couples perform a traditional ritual in which the bride, led by her mother and mother-in-law, circles the groom either three or seven times, signifying that she is leaving her parents' home and entering her husband's. Some couples also have the groom, led by his father and father-in-law, circle the bride, symbolizing that he is also leaving his parents' care to establish a new household with his new wife.

The rabbi now may say a few words about the meaning of marriage and about the bride and groom. Someone in the wedding party says or chants the *Kiddush*, and the bride and groom each take a sip of wine.

The next part of the marriage ceremony is actually a betrothal or engagement ceremony. In talmudic times, couples were betrothed a year before they were married. However, since the twelfth century C.E., this older engagement ceremony has been incorporated directly into the first part of every Jewish wedding. In this engagement ceremony, the bride and groom are asked if they consent to the betrothal. Then the groom places a ring on the bride's right-hand index finger and says, in Hebrew and English, *Harei at*

A betrothal ring, Germany.

mekudeshet li betaba'at zo kedat Mosheh ve-yisrael:

הֲרֵי אַתְּ מְקֻדֶּשֶׁת לִי בְּטַבַּעַת זוֹ כְּדַת מֹשֶׁה וְיִשְׂרָאֵל.

"Be consecrated to me with this ring as my wife in accordance with the law of Moses and Israel."

In a marriage ceremony where the bride is giving a ring to the groom, she may repeat these words in Hebrew and English, substituting אַתָּה for אַתְּ and מְקֻדָּשׁ for מְקֻדֶּשֶׁת, or she can say something equally appropriate. We call this "exchanging marriage vows." The betrothal segment of the ceremony is concluded when a participant reads the *ketubah* aloud.

The Wedding Ceremony: Marriage

Now the rabbi or cantor fills a second cup of wine or grape juice and recites or chants the *Sheva Berachot* שֶׁבַע בְּרָכוֹת, the "Seven Blessings." After the blessings, the bride and groom drink from the cup. In the final phase of the ceremony, the groom or the bride and groom together step on a glass wrapped in a napkin. When the glass is broken, everyone shouts "*Mazal Tov.*" The bride and groom may kiss. They are now officially married.

After the ceremony, the bride and groom go off together for a few minutes of private time before participating in the reception. This custom is called *yichud* יְחוּד, "seclusion." If the bride and the groom have followed the tradition of fasting before their marriage ceremony, during *yichud* they break their fast with a light snack. For most couples, *yichud* is an opportunity to spend a few quiet moments together to celebrate their new marriage privately before celebrating with all their relatives and friends.

Sheva Berachot

Rabbi (lifting a cup of wine):

בָּרוּךְ אַתָּה, יְיָ אֱלֹהֵינוּ, מֶלֶךְ הָעוֹלָם, בּוֹרֵא פְּרִי הַגָּפֶן.

We praise You, Adonai our God, Ruler of the universe, Creator of the fruit of the vine.

בָּרוּךְ אַתָּה, יְיָ אֱלֹהֵינוּ, מֶלֶךְ הָעוֹלָם, שֶׁהַכֹּל בָּרָא לִכְבוֹדוֹ.

We praise You, Adonai our God, Ruler of the universe, Creator of all things for Your glory.

בָּרוּךְ אַתָּה, יְיָ אֱלֹהֵינוּ, מֶלֶךְ הָעוֹלָם, יוֹצֵר הָאָדָם. בָּרוּךְ אַתָּה, יְיָ אֱלֹהֵינוּ, מֶלֶךְ הָעוֹלָם, אֲשֶׁר יָצַר אֶת־הָאָדָם בְּצַלְמוֹ, בְּצֶלֶם דְּמוּת תַּבְנִיתוֹ, וְהִתְקִין לוֹ מִמֶּנּוּ בִּנְיַן עֲדֵי עַד. בָּרוּךְ אַתָּה, יְיָ, יוֹצֵר הָאָדָם.

We praise You, Adonai our God, Ruler of the universe, Creator of man and woman.

שׂוֹשׂ תָּשִׂישׂ וְתָגֵל צִיּוֹן בְּקִבּוּץ בָּנֶיהָ לְתוֹכָהּ בְּשִׂמְחָה.

We praise You, Adonai our God, Ruler of the universe, who creates us to share with You in life's everlasting renewal.

בָּרוּךְ אַתָּה, יְיָ, מְשַׂמֵּחַ צִיּוֹן בְּבָנֶיהָ.

We praise You, Adonai our God, who causes Zion to rejoice in her children's happy return.

שַׂמֵּחַ תְּשַׂמַּח רֵעִים הָאֲהוּבִים כְּשַׂמֵּחֲךָ יְצִירְךָ בְּגַן עֵדֶן מִקֶּדֶם. בָּרוּךְ אַתָּה, יְיָ, מְשַׂמֵּחַ חָתָן וְכַלָּה.

We praise You, Adonai our God, who causes bride and groom to rejoice. May these loving companions rejoice as have Your creatures since the days of creation.

Rabbi or Assembly:

בָּרוּךְ אַתָּה, יְיָ אֱלֹהֵינוּ, מֶלֶךְ הָעוֹלָם, אֲשֶׁר בָּרָא שָׂשׂוֹן וְשִׂמְחָה, חָתָן וְכַלָּה, גִּילָה, רִנָּה, דִּיצָה וְחֶדְוָה, אַהֲבָה וְאַחֲוָה, שָׁלוֹם וְרֵעוּת. מְהֵרָה, יְיָ אֱלֹהֵינוּ, יִשָּׁמַע בְּעָרֵי יְהוּדָה וּבְחוּצוֹת יְרוּשָׁלַיִם קוֹל שָׂשׂוֹן וְקוֹל שִׂמְחָה, קוֹל חָתָן וְקוֹל כַּלָּה, קוֹל מִצַּהֲלוֹת חֲתָנִים מֵחֻפָּתָם וּנְעָרִים מִמִּשְׁתֵּה נְגִינָתָם. בָּרוּךְ אַתָּה, יְיָ, מְשַׂמֵּחַ חָתָן עִם־הַכַּלָּה.

We praise You, Adonai our God, Ruler of the universe, Creator of joy and gladness, bride and groom, love and kinship, peace and friendship. O God, may there always be heard in the cities of Israel and in the streets of Jerusalem: the sounds of joy and of happiness, the voice of the groom and the voice of the bride, the shouts of young people celebrating, and the songs of children at play. We praise You, our God, who causes the bride and groom to rejoice together.

Why We Break a Glass at the Wedding

The breaking of the glass is a medieval custom with different interpretations. Below are two of many explanations:

1. Many legends, Jewish and non-Jewish, have been written about evil spirits who come to weddings. It has been said that evil spirits are attracted to celebrations to harm the bride and groom. The noise of the breaking glass and the shouting of "*Mazal Tov*" were thought to scare away these evil spirits.

2. We break the glass to remind us of the destruction of the Holy Temple in Jerusalem. This act teaches us to acknowledge that life has times of great sorrow even during a time of great joy.

When a Marriage Fails—Divorce

It may seem odd to include a discussion of divorce in a chapter on marriage. However, it is a reality of life that despite the best efforts of both partners, some marriages end in divorce. Jewish tradition has always recognized this possibility. Just as Jewish marriages are governed by rules that involve a legal contract, the *ketubah*, Jewish divorce requires a legal document known as a *get* גֵּט. *Get* is a Hebrew word meaning "certificate," with the additional meaning of a document that ends a relationship.

Before seeking a divorce, a couple is encouraged to make every effort to stay together to rebuild their relationship. However, divorce is sometimes inevitable. According to Jewish law, a *get*, a "bill of divorce," is required for the dissolution of a Jewish marriage. After a Jewish divorce, both husband and wife are free to marry again.

A Turkish Jewish wedding, Ottoman Empire, 1862.

97

SUMMARY

In this chapter we have seen that Jewish marriage, a very distinctive part of the life cycle, has its own unique customs. You are probably many years away from marriage. Nonetheless, it is never too early to learn about the holiness of marriage and particularly of Jewish marriage. You may now understand better why your parents and other adults have sought to impress upon you the significance of this step.

Not all aspects of the life cycle are happy. Just as Judaism teaches us how to rejoice, it also teaches us how to mourn. In the next chapter we shall look at Jewish beliefs and observances regarding death and mourning.

CHAPTER NINE

DEATH AND MOURNING

Sing Many Songs That You May Be Remembered

Once upon a time, there was a girl named Lynn, who lived with her parents and her grandmother Bessie. Lynn's Grandma Bessie was different from the grandmothers of Lynn's other friends. Grandma Bessie had grown up in a small town called Skvira, in Ukraine, a country that had once been part of Russia.

Lynn's grandmother loved to talk about her childhood in Skvira. Lynn especially loved to hear about the foods her grandmother missed from "the old country." According to Grandma Bessie, the chocolate candy was like no other chocolate in the world. And there was a smoked fish called kapchanka. When Bessie said "kapchanka," she smacked her lips and smiled broadly.

Bessie and all the Jews in Skvira spoke both Russian and Yiddish. Even though Bessie had lived in America for a long time and spoke English very well, she still spoke with an accent, and sometimes she spoke Yiddish with Lynn's mother, when they had secrets they didn't want Lynn to discover.

"Why did you speak both Russian and Yiddish?" Lynn asked her grandmother one day. Bessie explained that Yiddish was a language spoken by Jews in Russia and many other countries so that if they traveled outside their own countries, they could talk to other Jews.

"Could you teach me something in Yiddish?" Lynn asked.

"Uff course," her grandmother said, in her special way. "I'll teach you a song my mother taught me when I was a little girl. It's called *Oyfen Pripichick*, and it's about Jewish children learning the *Aleph-*

Bet." Then she sang the Yiddish song in a sweet, soft voice.

Lynn listened carefully. Then her grandmother said the words slowly, and Lynn repeated them. Soon she knew the whole song by heart.

Lynn loved this song. She didn't know exactly what every word meant, but that didn't matter to her. She was just happy that she could sing a song in her grandmother's language.

Singing the song made Lynn feel as if her grandmother were nearby. Some of the words were very difficult and felt foreign in her mouth. When she sang them, she sometimes felt as if she were her grandmother as a little girl living in Skvira. When she and her grandmother sang the song together, it was as if they were having a conversation in Yiddish—almost like two young girls living in another time and place. When Lynn went away to summer camp for the first time and felt lonely, she sang herself to sleep with the song. In her heart she could feel her grandmother singing with her, and she felt her loneliness disappear.

In time, Lynn grew up, got married, and had a child of her own, a little boy she named David. One day she took David to see his great-grandmother. Lynn said to her son, "When I was your age, Grandma Bessie taught me a Yiddish song. Would you like to hear us sing it?" And she and her grandmother sang *Oyfen*

Pripichick for David. Then, together, they taught him the song so he could sing it with them.

Time went by. Lynn's grandmother grew very old, and one sad day, she died. Lynn knew that her grandmother had lived a long, full life, but she was still sad to have to say good-bye to her. At the funeral, many people said nice, comforting things, but none of the things they said took away Lynn's feeling of loss. She wanted her grandmother to come back, and she knew that could never happen.

One night, when she was in bed, Lynn thought about the day her grandmother had taught her *Oyfen Pripichick*. She thought about the many times they'd sung it together. She thought about the day they had taught the song to David.

Suddenly, she heard a soft voice singing in the next room. It was David. He was singing the song. As Lynn listened to his sweet voice, she began to smile, and a tear rolled down her check. Finally she felt comforted for the first time since her grandmother's death. She knew that someday David would teach the song to his children and would tell them about his great-grandmother, who taught him the song. Through that simple song, Bessie would always be part of their family.

JO DAVID

101

Among the most important characteristics of Judaism are the many ways we remember our loved ones who have died. From a very early time, Jews have understood that memory has the power to heal a broken heart and help us maintain our connection with those we love even after their death.

We have specific prayers to remember those whom we have lost. We have a special part of every worship service devoted to remembering. We have even created rituals of remembrance for Yom Kippur יוֹם כִּפּוּר, Shemini Atzeret שְׁמִינִי עֲצֶרֶת, Passover, and Shavuot. We believe that death has to be faced and accepted for us to live stronger, more content lives.

Often our first confrontation with death is when we are young. We see flowers picked the previous day lose their color and wilt. Perhaps a favorite pet has died; perhaps a relative has died of illness or old age.

Do you remember the first time you had such an experience? What did your parents say to you? How did they comfort you? It is difficult for parents to explain death to their young children because parents fear that children will be frightened by the concept that everything that lives must eventually die. For this reason, parents often create a story that may satisfy a young child but probably would not satisfy you now.

We have included this chapter in our book because death is an important part of the life cycle. Understanding the Jewish view of death and the customs that have developed around it enable us to cope with this occurrence in our lives.

Jewish Beliefs about Death and Life after Death

Although many people try to avoid the subject, Judaism treats death as a natural part of the life cycle. All things pass; all that lives must die. While death is universal, it is a mystery. Why do some die young and others die at a very old age? What happens after death? Are good people who suffer rewarded after death? Are bad people who prosper punished? Do the good go to a "good" place and the bad to a "bad" place? Every religion struggles with these questions, and Judaism is no exception.

There are no definite answers to these difficult questions. Judaism stresses that we should perform good deeds while we are living. Throughout our long history, the Jewish views of life after death have developed and changed in many different ways.

Three Jewish Views of Life after Death

The Biblical View

The Bible does not mention different places for good people and bad people. There is no reference to heaven or hell. Although *Sheol*, a dark place beneath the earth where souls go, is mentioned a few times in the Bible, it is not a major concept.

The Middle Ages

As Jewish philosophy developed, the great rabbis offered new ideas of what happens after we die. One idea was that the soul, the special spirit that lives within us while we're alive, never dies. Some people believed that when the Messiah (the messenger of God who will bring about an era of peace and harmony for the whole world) comes, all the dead will be resurrected, brought back to life, and we will live forever in a perfect world.

The Modern View

Although modern Jews hold different views on life after death, many of these views still draw on ideas from earlier

The AIDS Memorial Quilt, in which Mark Feldman, the first member of Congregation Sha'ar Zahav to die of AIDS, is memorialized.

times. From biblical writings we learn that Judaism has held that good and evil will be rewarded in our lifetime. Therefore, we have paid less attention to life after death than to living a good life in the present. The Talmud states, "Better one hour of repentance and good works in this world than all the life in the world to come" (*Pirke Avot* 4:17). Of course, no one really knows what happens after we die. But we do know that we continue to "live" after death through the memories of the living.

Jewish Funeral Customs

The period of time between the death and burial of a Jewish person is filled with many special rituals and practices. Two principles guide most Jewish funeral and mourning customs: helping the mourners adjust to the death of a loved one and showing respect for the person who has died.

Everything that happens between the time a person dies and the time the person is buried is designed to show *kevod hamet* כְּבוֹד הַמֵּת, "honor for the dead." The concept of *kevod hamet* is one of the greatest *mitzvot* in Judaism. A primary aspect of this *mitzvah* is handling the dead body with love and respect. When a Jewish person dies, the body is taken to a funeral parlor, where it is washed and dressed for burial. These tasks may be performed by employees of the funeral parlor or by members of a *chevrah kaddisha* חֶבְרָה קַדִּישָׁא, a specially trained volunteer group that prepares the body for burial according to Jewish law. Because some Jews believe the body should not be

unattended from the moment of death until the time of burial, they follow the traditional practice of having someone sit with the body, reading psalms, until the funeral begins.

A water scoop used by members of the chevrah kaddisha *for washing the body of the deceased, Poland, 1655.*

The Acafoth *or the seven turns around the coffin, Bernard Picart, 1723, engraving, printed in black. Israel Solomons Collection. Photography by Lelo Cater.*

The body is washed, dressed, and placed in a coffin, which is then closed. Traditional Judaism believes that the body should be allowed to decompose as quickly as possible. Thus, embalming, which is a way of slowing down the process of decay that begins when the body dies, is prohibited. For the same reason, some Jews follow the tradition of using a simple pine coffin.

It is Jewish custom to bury a person as soon after death as possible, preferably within twenty-four hours. This custom developed in biblical times for health reasons. Today we continue the custom of quick burials, but we are more concerned with honoring the dead and helping the grieving family members say their final farewells with as little delay as possible. Sometimes it is necessary to delay a funeral because family members coming from a distance need time to travel. Another reason to delay a funeral stems from the traditional prohibition against holding funerals on Shabbat, Yom Kippur, or the first or last days of a Jewish festival. The rabbis taught that a sad event should not diminish a happy or sacred occasion. However, when Jews choose to celebrate the first two days of festival holidays, funerals may be held on the second day.

Funeral services can take place at a funeral chapel, in a synagogue, or at the graveside. If a synagogue or chapel service is performed, the immediate family and close friends then proceed to the graveside for the burial.

Understanding a Jewish Funeral

The order of a Jewish funeral and most mourning customs have their roots in ancient times.

Just before the service, mourners in the immediate family—parents, children, spouses, and siblings—cut or tear an article of their clothing as an outward sign of

World leaders gather to pay their respects to the late Israeli Prime Minister Yitzhack Rabin.

a broken heart. Some Jews follow the custom of cutting a piece of black ribbon that has been attached to their clothing. The ceremony of tearing or cutting the garment or ribbon is called *keriah* קְרִיעָה. Custom dictates tearing the garment or placing the cut ribbon on the left for mourning a parent and on the right for mourning another relative. The mourners wear the ribbon or cut garment for at least seven days after the funeral; some wear it for thirty days.

Psalms, songs, and poetry from the Bible are used as words of comfort during the funeral service. A rabbi, cantor, or adult Jew conducting the service will read or chant some psalms. Psalms 23, 49, 90, and 91 are traditionally included.

After the psalms are read, someone gives a *hesped* הֶסְפֵּד, "eulogy." This is usually the person conducting the service or a family member or close friend of the deceased. Sometimes several people may speak, sharing their loving memories of the deceased. In this way, they praise the person who has died, honor the person's memory, and bring comfort to the family and friends who are in mourning.

A Jewish burial, Amsterdam, eighteenth century.

After the eulogy or eulogies, everyone sings the prayer *El Malei Rachamim* אֵל מָלֵא רַחֲמִים, "God, full of compassion." This prayer asks God to give rest to the soul of the deceased and mentions the person's Hebrew name.

If the service is in a synagogue or chapel, the family accompanies the coffin to the cemetery, where the service is concluded. If the service is at the graveside, everyone—traditionally, a *minyan* is required—recites the *Mourner's Kaddish* קַדִּישׁ יָתוֹם, and the service is concluded.

Burying a loved one is the responsibility of the immediate family. Today many Jews prefer to have professionals fill in the grave, and this has become an accepted custom. However, we have retained the practice of showing *kevod hamet* by having family members put a bit of earth into the grave after the coffin has been lowered so that this last act of kindness is not done by a stranger. This is done by placing some earth on the back of a shovel and putting the earth into the grave. The person then lays down the shovel, and the next person picks it up. These traditions developed to avoid giving the impression that the family wishes to bury the dead person quickly.

The *Mourner's Kaddish* is a special prayer that we recite in honor of someone who has died. It is significant that the *Kaddish* makes no mention of death. It is a prayer that praises God. We say *Kaddish* to show that even in our grief, we accept God's presence in our lives.

יִתְגַּדַּל וְיִתְקַדַּשׁ שְׁמֵהּ רַבָּא בְּעָלְמָא דִּי־בְרָא כִרְעוּתֵהּ, וְיַמְלִיךְ מַלְכוּתֵהּ בְּחַיֵּיכוֹן וּבְיוֹמֵיכוֹן וּבְחַיֵּי דְכָל־בֵּית יִשְׂרָאֵל, בַּעֲגָלָא וּבִזְמַן קָרִיב, וְאִמְרוּ אָמֵן.

Let the glory of God be extolled and God's great name be hallowed in the world whose creation God willed. May God rule in our own day, in our own lives, and in the life of all Israel, and let us say Amen.

יְהֵא שְׁמֵהּ רַבָּא מְבָרַךְ לְעָלַם וּלְעָלְמֵי עָלְמַיָּא.

Let God's great name be blessed for ever and ever.

יִתְבָּרַךְ וְיִשְׁתַּבַּח, וְיִתְפָּאַר וְיִתְרוֹמַם וְיִתְנַשֵּׂא, וְיִתְהַדָּר וְיִתְעַלֶּה וְיִתְהַלָּל שְׁמֵהּ דְּקוּדְשָׁא, בְּרִיךְ הוּא, לְעֵלָּא מִן כָּל־בִּרְכָתָא וְשִׁירָתָא, תֻּשְׁבְּחָתָא וְנֶחֱמָתָא דַּאֲמִירָן בְּעָלְמָא, וְאִמְרוּ אָמֵן.

Beyond all the praises, songs, and adorations that we can utter is the Holy One, the Blessed One, whom yet we glorify, honor, and exalt, and let us say Amen.

יְהֵא שְׁלָמָא רַבָּא מִן־שְׁמַיָּא וְחַיִּים עָלֵינוּ וְעַל־כָּל־יִשְׂרָאֵל, וְאִמְרוּ אָמֵן.

For us and for all Israel, may the blessing of peace and the promise of life come true, and let us say Amen.

עֹשֶׂה שָׁלוֹם בִּמְרוֹמָיו, הוּא יַעֲשֶׂה שָׁלוֹם עָלֵינוּ וְעַל־כָּל־יִשְׂרָאֵל, וְאִמְרוּ אָמֵן.

May the One who causes peace to reign in the high heavens cause peace to reign among us, all Israel, and all the world, and let us say Amen.

Psalms are read during the funeral service because of the comfort that their beautiful words bring to mourners. Psalm 23 is the best known because it is used by both Jews and Christians.

> God is my shepherd, I shall not want.
> You make me lie down in green pastures,
> Lead me beside still waters, and restore my soul.
> You lead me in straight paths for the sake of Your name.

> Even when I walk through the valley of the shadow of death,
> I shall fear no evil, for You are with me;
> Your rod and Your staff, they comfort me.
> You have set a table before me in the presence of my enemies;
> You have anointed my head with oil; my cup overflows.
> Surely goodness and mercy shall follow me all the days of my life;
> And I shall dwell in the house of God for ever.

Shivah

While the Jewish funeral and burial take place outside the home, most Jewish mourning customs that follow the funeral are centered in the home. After the funeral, the family and friends return to the mourner's home for a traditional meal called a *seudat havra'ah* סְעֻדַּת הַבְרָאָה, a "meal of consolation," usually prepared by the family and friends. It is customary to serve lentils, hard-boiled eggs, bread, and dairy foods. Because both lentils and eggs are round, they symbolize the cycle of life.

For the next seven days, the immediate family sits *shivah* שִׁבְעָה at home. The Hebrew word *shivah* means "seven."

However, this initial seven-day period of mourning can be shortened by a festival. The *shivah* period begins immediately after the funeral and ends seven days later after the daily *Shacharit* שַׁחֲרִית, the Morning Service.

During the *shivah* period, it is traditional for mourners to sit on low benches or boxes. It is not clear how this very old custom of sitting close to the ground started but because we sit close to the ground, the phrase "sitting *shivah*" came to be used for this phase of mourning. Today many Jews do not follow this custom.

When mourners sit *shivah*, their friends and relatives visit and console them. This is called "paying a condolence call." The

Talmud (*Sotah* 14a) teaches that the tradition of consoling mourners is based on Genesis 25:11: "After the death of Abraham, God blessed his son Isaac." According to Judaism, people should model their behavior on what God does. The Talmud explains that just as Isaac was consoled by God's blessing, so are we commanded to bring comfort to those we care about by visiting them after the death of a loved one. Another source for the custom of paying a condolence call comes from the Book of Job 2:13, in which Job's three friends "sat down with him upon the ground…for they saw that his grief was very great."

Besides consoling the mourners, a visitor may be asked to take part in a *shivah minyan* שִׁבְעָה מִנְיָן. This is a regular morning and evening prayer service during which the mourners say *Kaddish*. Since traditional Jewish practice requires a *minyan*—a group of ten Jewish men—to say *Kaddish*, the prayer service is conducted in the house of mourning to enable the mourners to say the prayer. We still use the term *shivah minyan* for that service. Reform and Conservative Jews count both men and women as part of a *minyan* and do not require a *minyan* to recite *Kaddish*.

Things Not Done during the Shivah Period

According to traditional Jewish custom, people sitting *shivah* refrain from…

* leaving the house, except to go to synagogue on Shabbat.

* working or conducting any kind of business.

* showing concern for their physical appearance.

* participating in all forms of entertainment.

* wearing new clothes.

* wearing leather shoes.

After the Shivah Period

After the initial *shivah* period, formal mourning continues for an additional twenty-three days. The total number of days of traditional mourning is called *sheloshim* שְׁלֹשִׁים, the Hebrew word for "thirty": seven days of the *shivah* period plus twenty-three additional days.

During *sheloshim*, mourners may return

to work or school, but they continue to recite the *Kaddish* in a *minyan* in a synagogue; they do not go to parties, especially those with music or dancing; and they stay away from gatherings that are purely social.

The end of *sheloshim* marks the end of formal mourning unless one is mourning a parent. If one is mourning a parent, *Kaddish* is recited for an additional ten months according to traditional custom and eleven months according to Reform custom.

Headstones with niches for ceremonial candles.

Within the year of formal mourning, the family erects a tombstone. It has become an American Jewish tradition to have a formal unveiling ceremony, at which time family and friends visit the grave and view the newly erected headstone. At the unveiling ceremony, people may read psalms or speak about the deceased. The stone is revealed, and those

present recite the *El Malei Rachamim* and *Kaddish*. Anyone can officiate at an unveiling; a rabbi or cantor is not required.

After the unveiling, it is customary to visit the gravesite periodically, especially on the anniversary of the person's death. Frequent visits are not encouraged because Judaism discourages excessive mourning. Generally, Jews do not leave flowers on a gravesite. The custom of placing small stones on top of the headstone to show that loved ones have visited the grave has no religious basis.

Yahrzeit and Yizkor

Jews regularly remember those we loved and lost by observing *yahrzeit*, a German/Yiddish word meaning "year's time." It refers to the custom of commemorating the anniversary of a loved one's death (the date of the actual death, not the burial). Traditional Jews observe the Hebrew calendar date of death while many Reform Jews observe the secular calendar date. To mark the *yahrzeit* of a loved one, it is customary to light a twenty-four-hour *yahrzeit* candle at sundown the day before the date of the person's death, to recite *Kaddish* in the synagogue on that day or on the Sabbath closest to the date, and to visit the cemetery at about that time. In addition, it is traditional to give *tzedakah*, perform acts of *gemilut*

Jahrzeit at the Front, *Moritz Oppenheim, painting, Germany, nineteenth century.*

chasadim, and study the Torah.

Yizkor יִזְכֹּר, a special memorial service, is another way Jews regularly remember those who have died. *Yizkor* means "May God remember." It is part of the worship service on Yom Kippur, Shemini Atzeret (the eighth day of Sukot), and the last days of Pesach and Shavuot.

Ethical Wills

Most of this chapter focuses on how to comfort mourners and how to honor the dead. Furthermore, there is a way that people before they die can help their loved ones remember them after they have died. While a "will" is a document explaining what individuals want to happen to their possessions after death, an "ethical will" is an individual's "prescription" for living a good life. The ethical will, a tradition that has existed for hundreds of years, can take the form of a letter or a piece of original art work. Through ethical wills, Jews leave a legacy of their memories, ideas, or helpful advice for their loved ones. An ethical will is a gift to children or grandchildren while its author is still living.

A yahrzeit *lamp.*

Judaism teaches that death is a part of life. Just as there are special rituals to help us celebrate happy times, there are also special rituals to help us through difficult times. The primary goals of Jewish funeral and mourning rituals are to honor the dead and support the mourners.

Judaism teaches that death is not the end of a loved one. We can keep alive our love through memory, prayer, festival observances, and understanding that love does not die when the body dies.

INDEX